More praise for *Stepping on Cheerios*

"In *Stepping on Cheerios*, Betsy Singleton Snyder describes her daily struggles of having four babies in diapers and dealing with a health scare at the same time. Her humorous and inspiring spiritual journey is one of healing and finding grace amid the daily turmoil. I recommend this lovely book to mothers and fathers." — **Ginger Beebe**, former first lady of Arkansas

"Warm. Funny. Charming. Insightful. Compassionate. Grace-filled. A book for new mom, grandmoms, anyone and everyone raising kids." —**Bishop Janice Riggle Huie**

"Where was this wit and grace when I was a young mother? I would have kept Betsy Singleton Snyder's book on my nightstand, ready to remind myself that I am a person, a child of God, and a work in progress. Snyder writes with an uncanny combination of objectivity and tender intimacy when she talks about how our own messy faith in Jesus and in our families can be closely related." —**Diana Brown Holbert**, MM, MDiv, DMin

"I can easily recommend this book as the thoughtfully clever rumblings of a mind committed to ministry, to motherhood, to being a loving and supportive wife all at the same time. And it is just good fun to read. So have at it, sisters, and may a brother or two join in the fun, too!" —**John C. Holbert**, Lois Craddock Perkins Professor of Homiletics Emeritus, Perkins School of Theology

"When Betsy contacted me to see if I would do an advance review of her book *Stepping on Cheerios*, I thought, *I don't have time for this*. After all, I too am a pastor, and though I am raising only one boy and not four like she is, I do have two churches, which is like having fraternal twins who are all ages simultaneously. But I have such deep respect for Betsy, I said yes anyway. Then I got my copy, which came when year-end reports are due and new committees are meeting and semester report cards are being released. . . . but I picked it up, and suddenly I had all the time in the world to read it. Funny how your priorities can be so quickly rearranged by a breathtaking book. I say breathtaking because that is how her writing feels: frantic at times, as if you need to gasp for air, and peaceful at times, as if you are listening to your child's sleep-breathing. In fact, she writes like parenthood is lived. At times her writing is fast-paced, almost chaotic, jumping from moment to moment as if there is not enough time to say all she needs to say, and then suddenly it slows and takes notice of all the beautiful details going on in our blessed and baffling lives. And like parenthood, she seems to exist in the past, the present, and the future all at the same time. In the midst of it all, Jesus is inhabiting. He walks across Legos, sits down at the wrong table, bangs a timpani of joy, all in the name of knowing us and loving us more than we could possibly imagine. That Betsy glimpses this and then articulates it so well and so real is a great gift to us all. It is worth reordering our day to swim in her story for a while, and in doing so, we will swim with ourselves and with Jesus." —**Rev. Dr. Michelle J. Morris**, pastor and contributor to the CEB Women's Bible

"This book should be by the bedside of every mother with small children to be read and reread daily as a devotional to keep connected and 'find God in the chaos and clutter of life.' Betsy Singleton Snyder humorously reminds every mother 'you never get it all done,' 'take sorta kinda breaks,' 'stop more,' 'be just you and nothing else,' 'locate and hallow the sacred family portals,' 'have family movie night as a spiritual practice,' 'bad stuff stinks but it demands notice,' and 'move through the earth.' A must-read for parents of small children. —**The Rev. Joanna Seibert**, MD, deacon, St. Mark's Episcopal Church, Little Rock, AR, author of *Taste and See: Experiences of God's Goodness Through Stories, Poems, and Food as seen by a Mother and Daughter*

Stepping On
Cheerios

**FINDING GOD IN THE CHAOS
AND CLUTTER OF LIFE**

Betsy Singleton Snyder

ABINGDON PRESS

NASHVILLE

STEPPING ON CHEERIOS
FINDING GOD IN THE CHAOS AND CLUTTER OF LIFE

Copyright © 2017 by Abingdon Press

All rights reserved.

Library of Congress Cataloging-in-Publication Data has been requested.

ISBN 978-1-5018-2725-9

17 18 19 20 21 22 23 24 25—10 9 8 7 6 5 4 3 2 1

MANUFACTURED IN THE UNITED STATES OF AMERICA

For the four boys and one guy who've made my life a living heaven:
Penn, Aubrey, Wyatt, Sullivan, and Victor

For Mom, who taught me about Jesus, being real, and loving when it's
inconvenient and hard.

CONTENTS

CHAPTER 1
A HAIL MARY

Then Mary said, "I am the Lord's servant.
Let it be with me just as you have said." Then the angel left her.
—Luke 1:38

When I find myself in times of trouble,
Mother Mary comes to me
—"Let It Be," The Beatles

I love football because it's so unpredictable. The weirdest things can happen, right? Such as lateral trick plays in which the chaos of the moment unfolds and the way a running back's smooth dodge can suddenly bring a team ahead on the scoreboard in the final minutes of a game. And there's that famous last-ditch effort when the quarterback drops back, his offensive line holds, and he launches that oblong ball spiraling through the air in a lovely, long arc. Wait for it; wait for it as it becomes clear. The ball is finally caught by a young man whose body is hanging in midair. It is a moment worthy of the ballet, when his feet touch down in the end zone. It is a Hail Mary. It appears both crazy and divine.

I've met divinely crazy. I caught a Hail Mary and then three more—*ahem*—quite late in life. I became a mother of four boys, including triplets, in two and a half years when I was forty-sevenish. I didn't dare drop the extras God had so gloriously and unpredictably thrown my way. I had expected ordinary, and I got extraordinary. Isn't that just like God *and* the insanity of football? You may not know what's coming in life, but it wouldn't be any fun if you did. Plus, you might refuse to participate because what if you got hurt or couldn't control most of life, which you can't? So let's face it. Authentic, no-holds-barred living creates risk, and there's no decent spiritual growth without these untamed ingredients. No one grows into mommyhood without her complimentary set of bruises and a strong need for a good age-defying hair-care regimen.

If we bracket the football motif, there are *other* reasons I'm not your typical mommy, as if any woman's story is cut out like a cookie. No, we women must have a few flashy sprinkles on top of our own lives. Still, my story is, at times, one of biblical proportions. Genesis unplugged, if you will. *Thank you, Jesus, for the drama, truly.*

For one thing, my perspective on parenthood has been shaped by my marrying someone who is older than me and who waited a long time to get married. Before we met, Victor had done everything, it seemed, except tie the knot and have kids. He'd been a marine, been a hospital orderly, worked with troubled kids, operated a gas station, become a doctor and practiced medicine, served in medical missions overseas, gotten a law degree at night, served in the state legislature, and run for Congress and won. Low achiever, huh?

We met while Victor was representing Arkansas' Second District. We dated for two years, and after extensive negotiations, I coaxed him into a family adventure. (I was about as subtle as my bird dog is when she drops a squirrel on the floor, all earnest in her pleasing look, not knowing she's blown it for the cute little mammal.)

I hadn't misrepresented myself. On our first date, I told him, in response to his question of what I wanted in life, that I wanted to get pregnant, have a baby, and dodge Legos. I didn't realize when I said it aloud that it would turn into such a whopper of an adventure.

We had our first child when Victor was fifty-eight. For perspective, he was born when Harry Truman was president, and I was born when JFK was president. George W. Bush was president when our first child arrived. That's *some* history and frame of reference. But don't be fooled. No matter how old you are, children keep you culturally relevant. Victor buys indie CDs (yep, he still buys CDs), and I download music by Katy Perry and Adele, which exists comfortably next to the music of

The Wiggles and *Les Misérables* and *Hamilton*. In seminary, I had a word processor, and there was no e-mail, let alone texting and Tweeting. Cell phones were ginormous and few people carried one. My spouse and I lived through segregation to the Civil Rights Act and the Supreme Court's ruling on gay marriage. We're really old, and sometimes people think we're the grandparents.

That's not all bad. God has a knack for picking older parents. Take Sarah and Abraham. God promised them children—as many as the stars in the night sky—in a conversation that spans about ten chapters of Genesis. It seemed to take forever, and there were a few twists and turns before they had Isaac, which—get this—means "laughter." I suspect that the name *Isaac* was chosen not only because Sarah laughed at the prospect of having a child at her age but also because in the grand scheme of life at any stage, faith is a big laughable leap, like a Hail Mary or, for some of us, a Hail Sarah. I discovered the shocking and glorious truth of funny faith when the doctor told me that my twins had turned into triplets. By the way, I didn't laugh when I got the news. In fact, I sobbed every night for a week. I'm glad I didn't know about the pending heart failure that I would have after they were born. I might have held a teeny grudge, but once in my arms, they were just so puppy-breath adorable.

Every future momma is stepping into uncharted waters. I think that's why I fell in love with Mary, the mother of Jesus, especially after the mission trips I made to Russia. The images or icons that hang throughout Orthodox churches there are painted, carved, and even made of metal. Each icon recalls a story, almost like an old family album kept from before you were born, to show you later, after you've matured, who you are. Your story seems minuscule, but God usually works with small, seemingly unimportant humans to change the world.

Why is that?

I think God cares less about obedience and more about imagination. God wants us to have a vision that's bigger than we are. After all, you can't get much more modest and less showy than an unmarried teenage peasant girl prepared to live the quiet life in Bethlehem. Mary is a model for pondering what big surprises God may be up to in our lives. She's a testament to an engaged relationship with the Divine Wrestler, involving the hard and profound work of listening for preposterous whispers from angels (Luke 1:26-38). That's what Mary did. She listened, pondered, and then let it fly.

And the next thing Mary did was run and tell her much older relative Elizabeth, who was also expecting a boy, this startling good news. Luke says their get-together was like a party, or maybe that's just how I read the story. They hugged, a baby kicked, and Mary sang a powerful anthem about the ways God lifts up the lowly and struggling. Then, maybe they went to shop for swaddling clothes and have a latte. Maybe that me-time let them know how important they would be to each other. Moms need one another, God knows.

Luke doesn't give us another story about them together, but we know these two mommas —and their sons—had a special bond. How else could they have made it through parenthood, but for support, faith, and coffee? Through the diapers, the Legos (I feel sure Jesus built with Legos and gave everybody his snack), the splashing in dirty river water (which was John's favorite activity; along with judging people a little too harshly), and the way those boys brought home just about anybody for supper.

We grown-ups sometimes forget how much childhood matters. It's filled with the sacred and is not to be missed when it comes around again during parenthood. And parenthood is the time of spirit formation in which we don't realize until later that everything kid-drenched around us was and is a gift.

Let that Hail Mary of momma-ness sail from your fingertips because blessed are those of us who savor the sacred moments of this beautiful, challenging work known as motherhood, both the boringly simple and the show-stoppingly profound.

CHAPTER 2

MY BIG FAT ANXIETY ATTACK

So, brothers and sisters, because of God's mercies, I encourage you to present your bodies as a living sacrifice that is holy and pleasing to God. This is your appropriate priestly service.
—Romans 12:1

Pay mind to your own life, your own health, and wholeness. A bleeding heart is of no help to anyone if it bleeds to death.
—Frederick Buechner

Think about the challenging task of becoming a spouse in the unexpected craziness of this world. When I've helped young adults who are preparing for marriage, many of them have been surprised that premarital discussions have brought them to tears. Of course they get weepy! We're talking about leaving behind single adulthood and the childhood mantle to launch into the "married people universe." Couples may be excited, even thrilled beyond their wildest dreams, but the unknown of a new, challenging role brings a feeling of loss as well. Whether marriage or motherhood, good and great changes may create not only feelings of sadness but also feelings of uncertainty, imbalance, and questions.

That is the path of this risky enterprise God has created called life. We get to experience and probe the full gamut of so much chaos and creativity, from the bugs my boys offer me for awe and inspection to the struggles I have about whether I'm breaking even on this mom path. It's a good thing God is so patient with self-obsessed me and my performance issues. I guess that makes me a good test case for how to lean into a motherhood anxiety attack.

My first long-awaited pregnancy was like a delicious drug. It could have been the hormones, but I think the whole experience was also embedded with a spiritual chip. I inhaled basically every minute of the anticipated "baby land," especially how I felt: thankful, creative, loving, joyful. I wasn't even sick, although I could *not* handle coffee—at all. My mom and sister warned me that roasted beans and their delicious aroma might become a smell and taste jettisoned, temporarily, for hot chocolate. They were right; this is a minor inconvenience that apparently runs in the family. Despite a long labor and C-section, after which I was handed a gorgeous, fat baby, I developed an almost immediate amnesia for the birthing discomfort and a new love—baby love—which almost made me forget how blue my husband's eyes are. Let's say they're a nice addition to the gene pool.

Pause the remote on this nearly perfect scene. Most of us know firsthand that life—marriage, pregnancy, children, family—never runs smoothly. As a pastor and a friend, I've known lots of expectant women who've had pregnancy problems arise, such as debilitating nausea, preeclampsia, and gestational diabetes. None of these complications are a joyride because they not only taint the pregnancy experience but also change your life forever. After getting off scot-free the first time, I made up for it the next round.

Being on bed rest may be the closest I'll ever come to any quiet, contemplative life in a religious order.

I'm not easily scared. I've been through political campaigns, including one during which my husband was likened to Pontius Pilate. People may not like him, but I'm the only one who can call him biblical names. (You big strong Samson, you!) Of course, I'm also a pastor—a woman pastor—which is not for the faint of heart either. Thank heavens my Bible has lots of women leaders in it and women whom Jesus loved—women who were accountants, masseuses, chefs, theologians, prophets, moms, wives, brides, widows, students, small-business owners, marketers, and evangelists. Thank heavens, too, for the many devoted Jesus followers who have not been snarky to me, continue to affirm my call, and never say my passionate voice sounds angry. I love y'all.

Politics and church work. I told you I'm not easily intimidated, but my second pregnancy *was* different, crazy different. Sisters, no one plans to have triplets. I promise that it never entered my realm of possibility. Multiples in threes *seem* mystical and curious. In my case, the whole event had the *Ripley's Believe It or Not* seal of approval because I'm also ancient, and being pregnant with triplets is called a high-risk pregnancy for *all* babies and moms. Anything can happen, and some very unpleasant things did happen.

First, I developed preeclampsia at twenty-nine weeks, six weeks before I delivered. During that six weeks I was on complete bed rest. To put this in perspective, I had worked outside the home in a busy profession for almost twenty years. Suddenly, I became a human incubator. The doctor ordered me to cease work communication with my church family of almost eight years and stay on my side all day, every day. I always pictured bed rest in cute pajamas, propped up on pillows, eating chocolate, and reading. That wasn't it. Sitting on the nest is physically and emotionally exhausting work. Go ask a hen.

I wasn't prepared for the boredom and confinement of bed rest either. Big adjustment. The only things I could do were sleep, eat a little (my stomach had relocated in my throat), and watch television, which, after a while, will drive you insane. This pregnancy was before the vast array of digital options available at our fingertips, but I don't think I could've Tweeted even if I'd wanted to. I did take some clumsy selfies of my Easter-egg belly and our toddler with my first iPhone. Hurray. Being on bed rest may be the closest I'll ever come to any quiet, contemplative life in a religious order. These changes in my daily routine may sound minor, but they weren't for me, since they were moving me closer to an epic identity crisis.

Here's the worst part.

After I delivered the triplets—all healthy boys—I had trouble breathing, actually taking in air. I was soon back in the hospital with a cardiologist standing in front of me, wondering aloud if I should be intubated. *He didn't just say that, did he?* I was in cardiac failure, a result of a virus that attacked my heart during pregnancy. I might improve, stay the same, or get worse. No one could predict.

Carrying that reality with me, I lived between bouts of crying and pumping breast milk. Looking back, the pump needed to go; but for nine weeks, it was a way of controlling a situation beyond my belief and acceptance, as well as bonding with my preemies. One of my spiritual growing edges will always be letting go. And you will never hear me say, "Let go and let God," because I like to argue with God. I think God likes it too. Check out those conversations with Abraham or Moses or that sassy Canaanite woman who challenged Jesus to help her daughter. Just like a mom.

By the time I was home, little of my life seemed familiar to me. I had one toddler and three infants, no pastoral work, an unhealthy and rather wrecked body, and zero privacy because—guess what—I needed every hand on deck I could possibly get.

My motherhood story may be on the extreme end of personal dislocation and stress, but that very same experience became a way to examine the losses and change in the light of God's grace.

Identity Change Is Scary, but There Are Ways to Lean into It

As might be expected from a pastor type, I'm going to throw out some obvious reasons that new motherhood—and being a parent *forever*—forces us to look at ourselves realistically, check our needy boxes, and reduce the fear and trembling. Most of the great God-people relationships in the Bible are about this sort of reckoning. Grab a double-shot espresso or your favorite tea and gather round. It's confession and communion time.

Give in to This Time in Your Life

I know, I know! There are so many moments, when it's all new, that you can't imagine ever souring on motherhood or the precious lotion-slathered bundle in front of you. I felt the same way. Sisters, all it takes is lost sleep, a chemical imbalance, too much advice from anyone and everywhere, perfectionist tendencies, and the tedium—yes, tedium—of being with small children every day to question who you've become. Often, I spend more time worrying about what might happen. Isn't that just like a trusting Christian? No wonder Jesus spent a lot of time trying to tell us that worrying our brains out won't help one single bit and that God will offer us not what we want (our old body back), but what we need (Luke 12:22-31). Then there are the days that the whole shebang goes off the rails. Way beyond tedium.

By the time we got all the babies home, Victor needed to return to work in DC, with a new Congress in session and a new president. My timing has always been fantastic. Thankfully, I'm sister-blessed. It's a fact. All of my brothers did extremely well in the selection of spouses, and therefore I have stellar sisters-in-law, real keepers. Aunt Becky volunteered to spend the night the Sunday night before Victor caught his mid-morning flight back to DC. In the wee hours of Monday, we sat around the nursery on the twin bed and in rockers, arms full, occasionally whispering. Aunt Becky casually mentioned this was going to be a great birthday. *What?* My sister-in-law chose to celebrate her birthday in our chaos. I should probably say she gives great gifts, like that mini lava lamp for my church office.

Next morning, as soon as Dad-da was out the door and headed to the airport, our toddler began to throw up. It was not neat either. Projectile. I was completely undone. I needed to protect the babies, clean the mess, stuff the soiled clothes in the wash, and get the sick one to the doctor, but there was a lot more to do at home with three infants. Becky sent me off anyway. I took my breast pump and my kid to the pediatrician. Yes, I did that.

There's nothing to be done for rotavirus, a gastrointestinal infection that causes horrible diarrhea. It takes three to eight days to run its course. I got home, shared the diagnosis, and moaned something like, "This is my worst nightmare." I tried to keep the sick toddler away from the babies (nearly impossible), their room, and their bottles. If I had gotten it, then where would the universe be? I was already obsessed about having hand sanitizer everywhere, insisting everyone have a squirt, as if I were offering a plate of bruschetta.

Smiling, Aunt Becky said, "Well then, you can check that worst nightmare off your list. That's happened and you can move on." This sister has stuck with us through thick and thin. She's like spiritual Gorilla Glue.

It was true that my sweet sister-in-law would walk out the door later, but she was with me then, lovingly reminding me that all this chaos was my life right now and that it wasn't the horror film I was imagining. (By the way, Aunt Becky has reduced my tendency to exaggerate, and I love that she tells me the truth I need to hear.)

Take Sorta, Kinda Breaks

One of the reasons I'm crazy about Jesus is his clear and deep desire to get stuck in the middle of our stuff. Whether our stuff is a food shortage with a lot of mouths to feed, bringing wine to a wedding, letting snotty-nosed and stinky kids crawl on him, or eating with outsiders who have been shamefully sidelined by polite, religious society, Jesus immerses himself in the chaos of human life. In Jesus, God shows us how wonderful it is to enter fully into this life and that sharing ourselves is what we are meant to do.

But let's put that in perspective. Jesus also got tired. He wasn't pretending. He needed some peace and quiet. People, Jesus slept! Have mercy! Remember the time the Lord fell asleep in a tiny cramped boat with a storm blowing and disciples screaming at him that he must not care one whit about their bohunkuses (Mark 4:35-41)?

Sound familiar?

First, that chicken on the sea story reminds me that caring for people 24/7 is exhausting. Amen! Second, our Bible story sadly illustrates that those of us who need all the help we can get frequently tell God, "Oh, you can't possibly understand! I'm sinking here." And there is God, right in our old rickety boat, maybe rolling his divine eyes at us. Thus and finally, our story says even the God who is with us, who became human to be with us, knows full well our momma-type exhaustion. Not only that, but God gives us a great example. Take a break. Snooze in a boat if you like. But find some way to disconnect, recharge, and reset.

When my boys were tiny, the cardiologist told me to start the exercise thing again. This wasn't about weight; it was about heart health. "Walk," he told me. While family or another helper watched the other three, I took a baby for a walk. In more than one way, it was healing. This almost-solitary walk in nature helped my heart beat a little faster and did wonders when there was absolutely no way to get out of the house otherwise. At first, we didn't own our van, the only vehicle in which you can really get four car seats. But no sane person leaves her house with a toddler and three infants anyway, not without backup.

Another respite strategy involved spreading blankets in the front yard as spring approached and sitting outside the house. It was soul oxygen. Often, Sister Gayle (my bio-sibling and second mother) or other helpers and I would sit on a quilt or two with babies kicking, and talk and have a front porch experience or a short stretch of lazy visiting. That's where Sister Gayle came up with our first family Halloween costume. "I know," she said, "they can go as the Big Bad Wolf and the Three Little Pigs!" We howled with laughter, but that is exactly how I dressed my sweet four for their first Halloween. I have the pictures to prove it to torture them later. Laughter works as a stress reducer. We memorialized our version of *Beach Blanket Bingo* by taking pictures too. We looked for ways to celebrate anything. Our first long-term babysitter for the boys—a funny, sweet, and spicy redhead—bought all of us Saint Paddy's Day shirts and Onesies for a casual photo shoot! For a time, no holiday passed without theme clothes. I'm in recovery now.

Eventually, "the babies," as everyone called them, got big enough to venture out more. By late spring, we had a van and spent Memorial Day weekend on the banks of the Arkansas River at a music festival. We spread the babies on a blanket and parked the strollers under a shade tree with a stuffed diaper bag and cooler for bottles. (Mastery of the chaos sometimes equals exposing it in public.) The hardest part of that outing—and many more to come—was answering curious people's questions about this large pile of infants next to us. *Are those triplets?* Yes. *Are they natural?* One hundred percent natural babies! No additives.

Although I had little time alone, I desperately needed a way to be out of the house, where, at times, I felt—and was—trapped, surrounded by too many people and an unending cycle of babies' sleeping, eating, pooping, and playing, a routine that rebooted every three and a half hours or so. And here was a real tough nut for me to handle: going to worship in a community was basically impossible. Fortunately, I was able to baptize my babies and preach a good-bye sermon for my church family, but the loss of my ministry and that community meant I had to find Sabbath in new ways. Some days a break came as rest in a quiet reading time with our toddler. Other times I sat on the floor in a pile of brightly colored baby toys, watching in wonderment as the babies sat up and pulled up, discovering the world around them. Everything was new and gave me new eyes too. At times, I allowed myself quick getaways during which my friends took me for a pedicure and some kind person actually washed, massaged, and put ointment on my feet. Indeed, those were Jesus moments too.

You Are Never, Ever Going to Get It All Done

Momma-Sister, you are never, ever going to get it all done. Almost every woman I know has a checklist. I bet you got it all done back in the day, didn't you? I'm with you, but let me put my arm around you. Not anymore. Stop it.

One of the great things about being older parents is that Victor and I already had established careers. We weren't juggling little children with graduate school or new jobs *and* lawn care, diaper disposal, bottle-making (twenty-four had to be made up every twenty-four hours), shopping, cooking, and all that other domestic stuff. Since Victor was gone a lot in the early days, we had a nanny and tons of family who helped us, which is not always the case for families with multiple babies. Volunteers regularly came over to take a shift. Frankly, it was a bugger just to deal with the enormous volunteer chart we kept on the kitchen island. Meals were a struggle because, often, there were lots of extra people in the house. Thankfully, my angel friend Cindy sent home-cooked food on Mondays, Wednesdays, and Fridays for six months! This was a huge help when I had several ladies holding my babies and I still wanted to offer hospitality. It's a Southern addiction, and feeding people happens to be biblical and spiritual. Just look at all those times God appears in the midst of a good meal and fellowship.

I have this great tea towel that says: "I see all these moms who can do everything. And then I think I should have them do stuff for me!" Please notice this humor on the hand towel is funny because we know it's not true. No one can do it all. Those of us who are older and have less to prove know *for real* that it's not true.

Some things are beyond Band-Aids.

However, let me confess that I, too, have succumbed to jealousy and guilt when confronted with a version of a perfect Facebook Mom. She's more accomplished than the lauded lady of Proverbs. This mom gets up at some ungodly hour—not judging—prepares breakfast, lunches, and snacks for activities; makes meals to freeze for later; and creates amazing birthday parties as evidenced by the awesome pictures. Did I mention her kids are geniuses? In fact, one skipped a grade. The guilt-ridden perfectionist that I am would love to hate her, but I can't because she is *soooo* nice. This I know: God loves her, and I truly wish I had her spirit and energy. But I am not her. I'm stuck with me, but God loves me, too, and you. And I take comfort in all the stories of how Jesus was constantly interrupted, pulled this way and that. His ministry didn't fit a chronological schedule. People had to wait on Jesus. He was human, too, remember? He lingered, visited with folk, and wasn't the best at time management.

Figure Out Your Soul Thing

Since I was an older new mom of four children and was also a new heart patient and a newly not-working pastor, I had to get a new soul thing. I would love to scrapbook, and maybe I will when I'm eighty and decide to divide up all the boys' bins. Or maybe I'll do what one mom did. This particular creative sister saved the bits and pieces that she took out of her son's pockets when washing his clothes, and, when he married, she put them on display in a beautiful glass lamp. I'm gushingly sentimental and have already put my oldest son's Lamb Chop, Monk Monk, and Baby James snuggle friends in a large glass lantern because he wants them near, even if he no longer cuddles with them. I love that sort of decorating because, on a busy day, I stop, look at those worn lovies and remember.

When the babies were about seven months old, our state newspaper set up a new mommy blog. I was invited to participate. No longer writing a sermon once a week, I missed that sweet torture. Sick, huh? That regular writing became my soul thing, and I would not have that collection of memories if I had not taken the time to write my thoughts, opinions, and observations of motherhood during that demanding season.

As our children have gotten older and are in school and activities, we must do a gut check now and again to decide what soul thing we can commit to. Right now, the boys have chosen ice skating. Apparently, they don't realize that we live in a hot, humid Southern state where ice rinks are hard to come by. I wasn't convinced we needed to go there, with lessons and all, but one of the triplets, Wyatt, would not let it go. I thought it was the result of watching *Frozen* too many times. I thought he'd lose interest. On the contrary, he did not lose interest, and all his brothers decided to give it a go. Within five months of starting his lessons, Wyatt skated his first performance at a Valentine's Day show. I let him give up tennis. Right now, ice is his soul thing.

If It Gets Really, Really Bad, Talk to Someone, Maybe a Real Therapist

Here's an important P.S. for when we spirituality-searching mom-people are stepping on Cheerios yet want to love our parent gig: we may need professional help. One day we may find that we are pounding on the bedroom window, motioning to a friend leaving our house—actually getting in her car—that she must come back into our house right this second before we run away to Antarctica.

That's really what happened. I was the one pounding and probably mouthing, "Don't leave me!"

The babies were about six months old when I was informed that I qualified for a full physical disability. I quickly realized I couldn't work with four tinies, but the doctor and people who know about such things said, "You cannot work at this time, maybe ever." This news coincided with having the babies for five days with no paid helper, coordinating and assisting volunteers, dealing with a surprise virus, and Victor leaving me—the nerve!—to go to DC for his regular workweek. I actually called my husband's office and told sweet Rhonda, the receptionist, that they—the people who worked for him—needed to get the Congressman home, like right now. Oh, my. I could not take one more person in my house or one more change in my life. I left him a message and told him to have his people call my people. (That is really funny now, seven years later.)

Without a shower, with hair sticking to my head, in dirty sweat pants, and probably with bad breath, I went to see a psychologist. After an initial evaluation, he suggested a spiritual therapist who loves purple. Bishop Betty the Best became my healer and the mentor of my own heart and emotions. (She's not really a bishop, but she does take care of lots of people, her flock of struggling, sweet souls.)

Sometimes a pastor or, in my case, another spiritual mentor is exactly what we need. But when your suffering is deeper and existential, we must use every tool that God gives us to get whole. That's what the Greek word *soza* means: "wholeness." A bleeding heart is no good at all if it bleeds to death, right? Some things are beyond Band-Aids.

Anxiety, neediness, and identity issues associated with motherhood can be a bridge to discovery. I have more days than I'd like to admit when I'm a hot-mess momma, surrounded by clutter, yelling boys, and all the stuff they build, tear up, and spill. Embarrassingly, I can be that person who hollers angrily, "Why is there blue toothpaste all over the floor?" My neatness factor is not OCD, but it's definitely on the radar. So neon-blue, glitter gel toothpaste smeared in the rug can freak me out, especially if it doesn't match.

But there is another me, the me who realizes that having blue toothpaste smeared everywhere is laugh-out-loud funny. Why is there even such a thing as blue toothpaste, and why am I buying it on a regular basis if it's being used as floor art? We have hieroglyphics, too, inscrutable pencil marks along the hall, and scratched furniture from various swords and ninja tools that missed their mark, thank goodness.

I kid you not. Less than one month after I splurged on the Pottery Barn Classic Everyday Suede slipcover for a chair in the den, there were tire marks on the cushion. I questioned the usual suspects, but who am I kidding?

I love this messy life. It will never be balanced or finished because that's the nature of creation, and God is always creating new stuff. Some days I will fit into my momma-life better than others, just as some days I follow Jesus better than others. I take comfort, though, and believe that Jesus really loved and hung out with women. Jesus strikes me as a porch sitter and a sweet-tea drinker, maybe even that guy interested in your cheese dip recipe. You know why? Because God always cares about our story. Indeed, God once told the followers, I have pitched my tent with you, right here in your campground, strewn with empty sippy cups, files of science fair projects, and the delicious smell of athletic clothes.

CHAPTER 3

THE PRODIGAL PACI

*"Or what woman, if she owns ten silver coins and loses one of them,
won't light a lamp and sweep the house, searching her home carefully
until she finds it?"*
—Luke 15:8

Bart: *You can have your dumb pacifier.*
Lisa: *See if we care.*
Bart: *We don't need pacifiers.*
Lisa: *We're big.*
Bart: *We watch TV.*
Lisa: *We're mature.*
Maggie takes out two pacifiers and gives them to Bart and Lisa.
—The Simpson

When your husband is in politics, you know politicians. Really. You know them personally, but you don't expect to get personal advice about home life from them. When Penn was a baby, Rep. Steny Hoyer of Maryland—*only* the Democratic House Minority Whip at the time, as in the second-highest-ranking member of Congress—phoned my husband about a bill that Congress would be taking up soon. My husband said, "Steny, if you don't know anything about breast-feeding, I don't *blankety* want to talk to you." Victor really said that, and I think, given my postpartum misery, he meant it. There I was, sitting on the bed, crying and trying to get this not-natural thing to happen gracefully. Steny Hoyer shot back, "I'll get three staffers on it right away!"

Our little domestic matter is probably not one you generally hear men in Congress discussing. Hands down, I think family is surely harder to negotiate than trade deals. This is my way of solving a trade deal real fast: *OK, you can have fifteen minutes of Minecraft, but that is it, Buster. You hear me, right?*

The women members of Congress are most likely another matter. I'd bet real dollars on their problem-solving abilities. I suspect they share advice on babies and grands in the women's room even while they're riffing on foreign policy.

While the guys may not share baby-sleeping techniques or breast-feeding how-tos with great regularity, back then, my husband annoyingly peppered his conversation with anything related to his firstborn child and, later, the whole pack. Victor liked sharing his family life with all his colleagues. I suspect it helped ground him while he was away from home. That was before most of us had a smartphone or FaceTime, so he stealthily carried the latest photos of all our children in his suit pocket, ready to whip them out for forced viewing. Poor Steny Hoyer. Poor Nancy Pelosi. Poor Mac Thornberry. Everyone, hide! Here comes Vic Snyder, thoughtful member of the House Committees on Armed Services and Veterans Affairs, with more baby pictures.

Honestly, his friends and colleagues were great. When we announced we were having triplets, one of our senators, Blanche Lincoln, who had twin boys, grabbed us in the airport and, with a huge smile, said, "I can give you two pieces of advice. Always accept help. Never turn it down. And second, always get two birthday cakes. Three in your case!"

I had added an army, and it was marching on me.

It's heartening to know leaders are real people who want to help change the world, starting with your little tribe. We received advice and letters from senators, members of Congress, presidents, and a vice president. It may surprise some people to know that Dick Cheney sent us a very cute Onesie with the seal of the Office of the Vice President. Thanks, Veep, for helping us all think more ambitiously.

Such encouraging words, letters, and gifts can be remarkable keepsakes.

But even more incredible and grounding for me are *the unending ways God is always searching to find us*, including the times parenting overload drives us near insanity and hiding. Hiding can be as subtle as not being authentic, not revealing our fears and doubts, and unwisely pretending we got this thing.

My dear sweet mother used a weird phrase when she thought a child might be fibbing. "Are you telling a Tee Wat-teeee?" she'd say, exaggerating the question with raised eyebrows. Don't ask me where that word came from. I think she read too much Roald Dahl.

We all have our secrets that we keep from one another, but there are no secrets from God. God knows when we're telling a big one. God knows when we're standing behind the itchy fig leaves not being real. I know when I'm kidding myself because it's exhausting: "Come to me, all you who are struggling hard and carrying heavy loads, and I will give you rest" (Matthew 11:28).

Jesus said give it to him, all of our luggage, baggage, and makeup bags. I have to remind myself of his generosity by listening to his stories regularly and hanging onto the saints in close proximity to me and mine. How's that for self-soothing? Although there's not a specific story about Jesus helping with the laundry or babysitting—frankly, those disciples were pretty helpless, like, *a lot*—we have treasured parables to unearth and hold to the light of day. Parables are pictures of God and us. In some photos we're closing our eyes or making a funny face or looking the other way. Sometimes, we're distracted, and sometimes we're not even in the picture. *Was that the back of my head? Who took that? I look awful!*

If you're suffering from a lack of needed reclusiveness and from a deep desire for grace, look at Luke's Gospel. He offers us three back-to-back versions of his well-known God-loves-you-so-much-and-can't-stop-searching-for-you story (see Luke 15). Christians commonly refer to the last in the trilogy, the climatic story, as the prodigal son because the emphasis seems to be on the naughty, wastrel son who spends his inheritance in true binge fashion. Prodigious spending. Yep, the youngest is having a cray time living it up out in the wide world. Then son number two hits bottom, finally aware that he's alone and naked among the pigs. We usually think of this parable as a forgiveness story.

My spiritual mentor, Friend Gayle, calls her dark days "the armpit of Sheol." *Sheol* is that great biblical word that I have chosen to interpret as "the Pits." Sitting in the armpit of Sheol, that younger brother realizes there's absolutely no reason for him to remain god-forsaken. *Why did he ever leave and try to do it all on his own?* He can have love, acceptance, and community. All he has to do is go home; clean sheets, a home-cooked meal, and a long, squeeze-till-it-hurts hug will be waiting.

After rereading these beautiful parables, I am rechristening the last story the Prodigal Parent. Why? Because in all three stories, and especially the last, God is the One who is obviously the imprudent and reckless One. God is the One who abandons all judgment, grudges, and possible resentment to lavish love on a child in need. Notice how God brings out all the stops in loving that lost child, from the best free-range beef to the David Yurman ring. (I might have held the ring back.)

God, you see, is there not only for the self-indulgent and world-weary but also for anyone who's overwhelmed by life. This God is for stressed-out women too. When you're lost in sleep-deprived nights, the thick fog of young children, and valleys of self-doubt about whether you're pulling off motherhood like you imagine you should, God is still with you. Sometimes those open arms are the arms of support already present in your life. And sometimes, God is waiting for you to say, "Help me."

Women in the Pits also need saints.

When I refer to saints, I mean people who know firsthand all about the Pits. I don't mean someone who is pious (those kind usually drive me nutty and threaten to undermine my rock-solid secure self) or a haloed figure whose prayers bring miracles or even a Mother

Teresa–caliber person. The way I see it, God can use anyone at any time because God is so beautifully gracious like that—reason one million and one that I'm not God. Just like that, God drops them into your needy midst to remind you that you—a flawed, limited human—are made for love, care, and community. Throwing a few gritty saints your way is God's way of saying, "It's not good for y'all to go it alone" (the Southern version of Genesis 2:18).

Dear Girlfriends, not to wallow in self-pity, but heart failure was one of those nasty little situations nestled in my very own Sheol-ish armpit. When it looked like I wasn't going to die right away, I needed help surviving each day. Surviving was being a late-forties mom with four children, two years and under, and a husband working in another town with my health issues thrown in. (Incredible kudos to the military families out there.)

Too many people assume pastors have a lot of stuff figured out. The main thing I have figured out is this: it's going to take my whole life to grow up, including completing all this hard work of loving God and neighbor. Loving people is

With four babies at home, I wondered what home actually meant because it was no longer a private sanctuary.

so hard. It's hard to love strangers, and most days it's even harder to love the people you live with. Having all these new people—little people, big people—in my house taxed any realistic attempt at mastering 1 Corinthians 13. I had added an army, and it was marching on me.

With that army came gear. Having gear for four young children is like being stuck in the toy aisle of a big-box store for eternity. It's fine to browse about ten minutes, but after that you need to go to yoga, Zumba, or whatever you can to shake off head-spinning clutter. If you're really in a bad way, nothing beats a red velvet cupcake with cream cheese icing. Not only did we have the not-so-standard three cribs and toddler bed, but there were also full-on gymnasium contraptions, swings, car seats, three—count them, three—high chairs, endless diapers, wipes, clothes, swaddles, bottles, charts, lovies, and pacifiers.

The green pacifier was my frenemy.

I had a thing about offering my kids chew toys. Introduced at the NICU, the green pacifier was something about which I was simultaneously appalled and curious. My firstborn had never shown any interest in a pacifier. Besides, it seemed like a thing we didn't need or want to initiate. I was concerned pacis would keep the babies from learning to self-soothe. While that's an important tool for any human, I'm embarrassed to admit that I was expecting too much of triplet preemies, like Baron von Trapp in *The Sound of Music* when he pulls out the whistle to get the kids in line—a real line.

I thought breast-feeding was the best way I could help my preemies, even though it wasn't good for me. I couldn't take the proper heart medicine, get the rest I needed, or let available friends and family help me. Someone should have pulled me aside with a "Hey, Hon, just a thought. Bad idea!" (Low whisper: *The good folks around me were letting me think I had some control.*) I ended up pumping for a while and had to use bottles anyway, so that every baby could be fed at the same time to keep on schedule, or we'd be feeding for two hours. Preemies like to take their sweet time when breast-feeding.

After our schedule was set, I relaxed my dogmatic opinions about breast milk and pacis and finally began to lighten up. Breaking news: my kind-hearted volunteers were not wet nurses. Most were past menopause. This wasn't going to be round two of my first pregnancy, lollygagging with my firstborn. I had to accept a very different situation. So I embraced my frenemy, buying three to four packages at a time, so that I'd always have a stash. I began to see the similarity of using a pacifier and fulfilling my own needs. *Help* is not a bad word. I needed some soothing, but where, when, and how was that going to happen? Probably the same way I searched for the frenemy when I was desperate. I looked anywhere my frenemy could have fallen: under beds, behind couches, in the laundry. The thing we hate to admit and need most was usually right under my nose.

Mom, Get a Neighborhood

With four babies at home, I wondered what *home* actually meant because it was no longer a private sanctuary. It had become Project Triplet, a three-teething-ring-circus and revolving door of church friends, neighbors, and strangers who signed up on the volunteer chart in the kitchen. The giant erase board, sitting on the island, loomed large.

This is what helpers walked into. The board was divided into days of the month, each day made up of three-hour increments, during which the babies were awakened, diapered, fed, maybe re-diapered, held, played with, re-swaddled, and placed back in bed; the mattress alarms turned on; a sound machine cranked; the curtains pulled; and the babies' consumption and elimination charted. Each baby was color-coded for convenience, wearing a particular color that matched his chart color and a bit of toenail polish to match. Wyatt was yellow; Sullivan was blue; and Aubrey was green.

Having all these children cuddled and cared for by others who came to my house, because there was no choice, left me frustrated with how to enjoy and bond with these precious, stinky messes. I wanted to do it all. I didn't want to hand them off to other people, but if I didn't, I might drop a baby, literally. The intimacy I'd had with my firstborn was replaced by community. Not lying. Some days my privacy felt like it had been stolen, so that all my vulnerabilities were on display.

So I started with training wheels. I had to learn that God was in the thick of my new family through my own family, friends, acquaintances I barely knew, and a few folks on the who-are-you-and-how-did-you-get-in-here continuum. Even though I might have chosen more privacy, I had a whole neighborhood of women who ate with me; sang to, rocked, and diapered my children; and talked to me. I grew to love them and cherish them.

Looking back, I had the kind of experience most women used to have when they gave birth at home. Other women living nearby came in to help the new mother in the weeks after, aiding her ability to return to her normal activities. Back then, one of the main offerings given to the neighbor who'd given birth was to prepare food. Today's casseroles sent to new parents are the downsized version, the leftovers of a tradition that once brought people together, face-to-face.

It makes me pause and consider why Jesus put such an emphasis on gatherings and meals. He ate with all sorts of people, pointing out to them that they were his family and that, from then on, they should help one another. When you eat together in community, you are not merely consuming food; you are breaking bread and becoming family. Jesus was the consummate eat-local foodie. If you're eating together, you're becoming family.

Although we don't know if Jesus ever attended a kid's birthday party or whether or not he babysat, he had *and has* an inclusive definition of neighbor and family. When parents came to him with their children, Jesus didn't tell them he had better things to do with his time or that parenting wasn't on his radar. Rather, Jesus blessed the children, and, I am convinced, this action still blesses all the parents who lift their runny-nosed, sticky, fidgety progeny into his arms (see Matthew 19:14-15 and Mark 10:13-15). When someone affirms by her presence that your kids need to be loved and that you do, too, well, isn't that person a gift from God? A neighbor. All those folks who helped take care of our babies took care of me too.

Surrender: Don't Do It Your Way

Suck on this one: loosen your grip. No one is going to do anything exactly like you. I know. You've got your special way of being in the world. God made only one of you. (I know my husband is soooo glad he lives with only one of me.) Whether it's soothing a crying infant, burping a child while holding him up or tossing him bag-of-taters-style over the shoulder, or making your one and only chicken tetrazzini, we've all got our styles. I beg you, Sister; unless it's dangerous, let it go. Your child is going to learn soon enough that there are diverse styles, opinions, strategies, and worldviews. By the way, that is a very good thing. Most days of mothering are learning to let go anyway. Breathe deeply.

Whether it's day care, a sitter, a mother-in-law, a family member, or a friend, no one can replace you as primary parent, but the job of parenthood is to give space to a world bigger than ourselves. Look at the long conversations Jesus had with people who were very different from him. Not only did he disagree with and debate the law with the religious authorities of his day, he also discussed his understanding of the spiritual life with people as diverse as a despised tax collector named Zacchaeus and a Samaritan woman. Jesus, in fact, made it a point to tell Zacchaeus they were going to eat together. Likewise, Jesus also pointedly walked right into Samarian borders to talk theology with someone different in ethnicity and gender. These encounters explain something important about God. God made diversity. God likes diversity. Diversity helps children. The breadth of opinion in this huge world is massive.

Did I say letting go was easy? The practice of surrendering our own perfection, our neatly barricaded emotional walls, or our insistence that we alone hold the keys to our child's happiness is a spiritual practice. Letting go is a habit we must practice if we are to cultivate surrender.

Own Your Needs

My boys are now about the size and age of Mowgli. Man cubs. They could probably figure out how to fetch honeycombs off a cliff for Baloo the bear. They make stuff. Endlessly. It's easy to see they're growing up, but the inner life is still and always will be a mystery.

That doesn't mean we don't apply the gift of discernment. What ways can we practice prodigious grace for ourselves and within our families? Not long ago, Sullivan, our middle triplet, was assigned a time-out after school for not having a good start that morning. Drama. His school has a color-coded behavioral system. He finished his day on the color orange, a behavior no-no. Upon learning that he had a lengthy time-out after school, he sobbed. And sobbed. Maybe time-out could be reframed as something positive and soothing. I said, "Let's do something to calm you. How about a bubble bath and time to your-self?" Sniff, snuffle, and head nod. I gave him a towel and bubbles and started his water. I checked on him once. After the warm bath, he put on jams and looked at books. He was a new man cub. I looked at him and, though there was no paci, saw that he had waded through his own trying, tangled jungle of needs and anxieties.

One evening at bedtime, Sullivan and Wyatt were discussing with me the two brief parables about the man who sold all he had to buy buried treasure and the merchant who sold everything just for that one precious jewel (see Matthew 13:44-46). After a moment, I asked, "What do you think of these stories?" Very quietly, Sullivan said, "God is the treasure." I tried not to stare at him, slack-jawed, because I had just heard the good news. *Oh yeah, I thought, I have to remember that when I get myself worked up about the dirty floors, the recent ant invasion in my kitchen, the laundry noise that is my background music, and all my momma-fears that threaten to overwhelm me. God is my treasure, and, incredibly, God believes I'm worth finding, too, even when I'm one hot, weird, anxious, weary mess. Could you just hand me that tissue?*

CHAPTER 4
LEGOS ARE A MEANS OF GRACE

To-do list: Buy estate. Make winter coats. Weave cloth 1st. Make family look good. Be strong. Get Michelle Obama arms.
—*Proverbs 31 #Twible*

I think I got it… but just in case tell me the whole thing again. I wasn't listening.
—*Emmet,* The Lego Movie

One Sunday, when my oldest child was about eight, he decided he wanted to get dressed a bit earlier and come to church with me, alone. That's how it started. For over a year, Penn had wanted consistently to distance himself from the rest of the pack and hang with the older crowd. By older, I mean people not his age. That might have been anyone not the age of his brothers and any people who were not his brothers. He regularly asks for a vacation from his brothers. *Please, Momma. You just don't know.* Well, I'm not sure that's fair. I live with them too.

So my little big man would start Sunday by snagging some coffee in the fellowship hall with his own cup, enough coffee, sugar, and milk to render the Starbuck's franchise null and void. I'm told he sat at the tables with the adults asking things like, "Now, Mike, what do you do?" He had friends like Mr. Steve who taught him how to work the digital camera for the online streaming of worship services. Penn was enjoying learning how to use his gifts and talents in a nurturing place. Yes, he's the pastor's kid—one of them—but he wants to carve out his own spiritual identity. I'm all for that.

As I was backing out of the driveway one Sunday morning, I paused and applied the brakes. I surveyed our yard, and I did not like what I saw. There was boy debris everywhere. They—meaning all of my kids—had taken the metal bowl that had once been the outdoor fire pit and placed it under the green recycling bin and "secured" it with rope. "It's a boat," I was told. Obviously. They had dragged bricks into the yard, left over from the time we turned the garage into a playroom and added onto the carport. There were pieces of metal wrapped in rainbow duct tape scattered around. I started rethinking the trendy-colored tape I'd bought because I didn't like the way it looked when I saw it littered throughout our landscaping. The bikes were also lying higgledy-piggledy across the yard.

"Look at that, Penn," I said with indignation. "What a mess! I bet our neighbors are sick of our cluttered yard. 'What kind of kids are we raising?' That's what they must think. We have got to get this stuff picked up."

He looked at me and calmly responded, "Momma, I don't think many people have four little boys. And they sure don't have four boys who like to get outside and create and invent things. Anyway, we're not doing a bunch of video games like other kids."

My son, the child-developmental specialist.

Parental tail between my legs, I had to agree.

By nature, I tend not to embrace clutter. I did fine without it for about forty-seven years. The problem is that no matter what bins or lockers or organizational system I use, nothing inoculates me from the mess of six busy people.

I confess that my aversion to piles of stuff probably mirrors the chaos going on inside my head: get the sermon done, take the cat to the vet, get gift cards for the teachers, have lunch with a pastor friend, reschedule dinner plans with friends, text a mom about a pick-up time for a son's friend, play tennis, drive to the ice rink and freeze my butt off during lessons, and, Oh Lordy, I forgot my puffy gloves, which is awful for my Raynaud's.

One night, while we were waiting for three children to practice for a spring ice skating show, I looked at Victor—both of us in our heavy coats—and said, "You know, when we had that ultrasound that showed we were having three more boys, I never pictured we'd be spending loads of time in an ice skating rink. Baseball, basketball, you know, something more organized maybe. But Zambonis, skates, guards, soakers, and skate bags that are used only half the time were nowhere in my future."

And why is it that the skate bags—a good theory of organization— are not used much? Because the Snyders have figured out that it works better for each boy to put on skates before we leave. We have to help get the boot comfortably in place, cinch them up, tie them, *then* leave for the rink.

I wish I was better at giving in to chaos, just letting it swirl around me like I'm in the eye of the hurricane. I can handle only so much of it, and then I default to a sweep of the house, picking up drained cups of milk scattered around, putting pillows back on couches, throwing books back in the cubbies, and, my personal love-hate favorite, trying to get a handle on the Legos.

For those of us struggling neat freaks who live with Legos every day, we know that those innocent-looking plastic pieces are more sinister than they appear. Duplos, the pre-Lego pieces for younger kids, were larger and more manageable. Loved them. Legos, however, look very large on the packaging, but don't let them fool you or intimidate you with those powerful scenes of super heroes and flying spaceships. Legos are insidiously tiny outside of their boxes and hyperfertile. Here's one of the greatest memes of all times: *I'll walk across Legos for you.* That's love, right there. All parents know they hurt like heck. Even Lego knows because they made a limited edition Lego slipper, given to 1,500 lucky parents—in France! How is that helping my tender tootsies in America, Lego manufacturer?

Sisters, every time we go to our favorite Lego store, I make a futile pledge. No more Legos. OK, no more Legos, for a while. I'm not going to collude with the interlocking brick system for at least forty days. Lego Lent. *Besides, do the math*, I remind myself. Take the number of Lego sets we own, the pieces in each, and the magic number of four boys, and what do you get? Too many Legos. They are under couches and tables, behind doors, in the laundry after washing clothes, on the floor in almost every room, and near my makeup. There are the mini figures, mini dolls—should be many figures and many dolls—Ninjago Spinners, Chima Speedorz, Elves' amulets, not to mention Star Wars, Minecraft, and Harry Potter sets.

But now we're in a public STEM school (science, technology, engineering, and math) and attend Lego League (robotic Legos!). How can I truly, in all good conscience, curse Legos when educators say these pieces of plastic have loads of potential for problem solving, creativity, teamwork, following instructions, and fine motor skills.

I need to play, and I want my kids to see me play, all my life.

I asked our third born, Sullivan, if his careful analysis of each building project was leading him toward engineering, architecture, or life as a contractor. "Not at all," he said, "I'm going to become a master Lego builder."

"You're going to design Lego kits," I assumed.

"No," he said. Slowly speaking, and so I could see his lips move since I obviously hadn't heard him, he clarified: *"I am going to build Legos."*

The reality is not as clear. I think he's more rogue than he realizes. Sullivan makes exactly what he sees on the box one time. One time he follows the instructions. Occasionally, he asks to preserve the vehicle, building, or flying object depicted on the box. Most of the time, though, at our house, nothing is allowed a long and happy life. At some point, it gets dismantled to be recycled into something less perfect and, probably, more original. Their creativity makes me feel insanely happy. I read about a blogger and extraordinary Lego builder from Tokyo who makes re-creations of popular food, like pizza and soft-serve ice cream. One morning I found *Star Wars'* Rey with her speeder boasting purple unicorn and spider hood ornaments. I would love a unicorn hood ornament.

I've noticed these creative mutations occur when anything on hand—not just Legos—seems almost obsolete or simply available for adaptation. Remnants of an old drum kit, a sound machine, a remote battery-operated car, or some of my dental floss. Fact: climbing our stairs to put up more of *their* stuff in *their* bedrooms, I found string lying on the floor, unwound from a tiny paddle. *Oh for heaven's sake!* It was my mint-flavored dental floss. I knew immediately my limited supply had been confiscated for creative scrutiny and to decipher how it unwinds and what creative treasure it might yield. The same disappearing happens with rolls of tape, toothpaste caps, and shoelaces. Once, my boys even tied their underwear together to make a rope. Another time they used yarn to build a booby trap in their room. Booby traps were very big for a while. I didn't even know my children knew what booby traps are. I guess that's partly what's fun about them. They are a surprise, secret mess, not a giant billboard mess.

Sisters, We Gotta Play More

Sometimes I have to remind myself about play since I am a serious adult who has experienced serious life events. What can look like a bunch of nothing can be the very ingredients of creativity and play.

Chaos and creation are so very close. I love the way the Book of Genesis illustrates the story of God creating. I'm convinced that was also play: "When God began to create the heavens and the earth—the earth was without shape or form" (Genesis 1:1-2a). But lo and behold, God fashions all this gorgeous stuff, and God really likes it. God sees how truly smashing it all is.

My momma loved the poetry of the great African American writer James Weldon Johnson. I still have her worn, illustrated copy of *God's Trombones* from 1964. In the verses of "The Creation," Johnson offers his own sermonic riff on how creation gets going, describing God's playfulness and creativity, standing there alone in the dark. God looks around and declares God's loneliness in the midnight of a hundred Louisiana swamps. And then God smiles, light breaks, and the darkness rolls away, so that God can declare, "That's good!" Since we are joyfully made in the image of God, we need to claim the ability occasionally to slay the chaos.

It's like the green floral party dress and accessories I recently wore to a spring event. I stood back and looked in the mirror at the necklace, heels, hair (freshly done), and toes in hot pink and thought, *Well, Sister, you took some chaos and made it work! It took some effort, but that looks good!* Boom.

I really do get overwhelmed by clutter. (Maybe I have a real diagnosis.) I get nervous and want to immerse myself in funny cat videos. But a pile of Legos on a table, that's someone's potential right there. Potential *all over* the place.

Believing that, I coach myself to let the chaos have its say, until here and there, I have to put my hands on chaos and start fashioning something different and new. Instead of Legos, it's those staples in my pantry. Maybe it's the butter, shortening, salt, flour, and cold water that are just screaming for me to get over my fear of failure. Make the blasted pie crust because it will be beyond belief tucked between layers of homegrown strawberries and real whipped cream! Tackling a pie crust freaks me out worse than Victor's yard designs, but it could be such a triumph. When I make flawless meringue, which is about once every other year for my Thanksgiving chocolate pie, I feel like dancing.

We are made in the Creator's image, and that ought to give us permission to let loose and dance. It grieves me when women hold back when playing. Your play is not my play. My play is not making pie crust every day either, but sometimes it is. Sometimes my play is framing pictures, planting in my tiny garden, listening to music, and singing out loud, even when my boys tell me to shush because they are embarrassed by my enthusiasm (which makes me sing even louder). Dissident, solitary singing is one way I play.

When I was in high school, I discovered tennis and played regularly through college, but then I became all adult busy and stopped playing. When my boys began to take lessons, I think I started mind-melding with our retriever, Nilla, and getting all ginned up when I saw a tennis ball. I just *had* to start taking lessons again.

Of course, a lot has changed, including major personal body shifts and alignments. Recently my backhand was so off that I told my coach my glasses were making it impossible for me to keep my eyes on the ball and follow the stroke all the way through. Plus, they just really mess up my foot work. He said it wasn't the glasses. OK. I accept his advice and feedback as he assesses my freaky throwback moves. But occasionally I produce a swing that is really quite pretty, quite good. And the ones

I miss—and that day I fell and skinned my knee—well, those things never happen if you don't play. I need to play, and I want my kids to see me play, all my life. God made me to play, and that was so generous of God to do that.

Stop More

I want to recommend something that mothers need much more of than we get or even allow: idleness.

When I traveled to Italy some years ago, I discovered that shop-keepers closed the doors and took naps during the day. And—oh my gosh!—so do other civilized people in this world. Uncivilized families (like my family) are way too busy too much of the time, which means we need more naps, less structure, and some mental wandering. I think we should have some specific off-grid, mental-wandering holidays.

Today, on this Grand Official Idle Day, you aren't allowed to think about what you did yesterday or are going to do tomorrow. If you do, your phone will blow up when you try to schedule anything in your calendar on this sacred and important day, and you'll be forced to sit at the Genius Bar for hours with your broken phone, unable to be idle. For what will it profit you if you have a magazine-worthy house that has sucked all your time and energy and has left you in mental anguish over laundry, sticky stuff, what's for dinner, or making sure your children are overly accomplished (see Matthew 16:21-28)?

Idleness can be a Sabbath, in which we're tuned in to what's hap-pening right now. Like that butterfly that just landed on my cone flow-ers. I notice not only the butterfly but also my cone flowers. In purple brilliance, they are stunning. I thank God for the cone flowers that were not more than a dormant clump of root ball below the dirt, waiting to bloom. As lame as I am at growing lilies, God still invites me to consider them, take note of them.

Sometimes I just leave Legos on the floor. I allow them to sit in idleness. Of course I'm tempted to pick them up or tell someone else to do it. I'm tempted to remind these people with whom I live that there are numerous places dedicated to putting their Legos, places I created that *mean* something. I resist saying that a dog might chew them, which would be very sad. I resist saying that Momma is so tired of picking up these tiny pieces. Poor Momma. These itty bitty blocks could be doing something or be hidden from view, but instead, they invite me to stop all my infernal, irritating need to get life just so—so neat and tidy.

I'm not good at idleness, but I think I need it. And I think it's an opportunity to be aware of God's invitations, which means I'm probably a closet Jesuit. I'm OK with that because I fell in love with Pope Francis when he washed and kissed the feet of a diverse group of young Muslims and Christians in prison that one Maundy Thursday. It's like he was kissing their boo-boos. Imagine that: the most important Christian leader, whom most of the world observes, stopped the customary upper echelon hobnobbing expected of him and got down on his knees, taking time to tend life's bruises. Take time to pause for the little encounters that are enormously important.

God Likes Legos

I can't always luxuriate in play or idleness, but Legos remind me that God is somehow involved in all our overwrought and cluttered lives.

Let's confess. *We* may forget that God cares about every last ounce of our lives, but God doesn't forget. *We* may not notice that God is in the pile of Legos at our feet and all the messiness that symbolizes, but that doesn't mean God isn't right in there with us.

Sometimes we need a "mac-and-Jesus moment," a way to understand that God can meet you in your extremely untidy house where the cuckoo crazies live and eat easy meals out of a box.

Think about how often God is so absolutely nutty to meet people wherever they are and whoever they are, for that matter. There was a man who was not in his right mind, but he didn't have to wait and get it all figured out on his own before Jesus was so *right* there! That's so comforting. Jesus was interested in him and cared about his current chaos (see Mark 5:1-20). That same Jesus showed up where an adulterous woman was about to be stoned and basically noted that we're all in the same sin boat and in great need of love, most especially when we have failed (see John 8:1-11).

The day came when I had to take the triplets shopping, which, unfortunately, was in public.

And, it's just like God to show up where you're working your tail off. Jesus met people in their workplaces and in their homes. Jesus came to Peter, James, and John, who were busy fishermen, trying to mend their nets. Jesus met a Samaritan woman who was trying to get water for her home. Jesus met Matthew in his little tax booth.

Way too often, we think God is locked up in the church or the synagogue or mosque. In my tradition, God became flesh and wandered around like some lost woman in Target, constantly getting sidetracked on this aisle or that aisle, by this person or that, juggling a giant cart of human needs. God is a very involved parent, so don't ever think you've got to line those rubber duckies up in a neat row before God is swimming with you.

Before I returned to work, I shopped at a Huge and Frightening Discount Store, where I often felt overwhelmed by the choices. Most of the time, I wanted one thing and one thing only: to get out of there as soon as possible so I could get home.

The day came when I had to take the triplets shopping, which, unfortunately, was in public. Big Boy was in school. It was the triplets' first time to go on a shopping haul with Momma at the Huge and Frightening Discount Store. Because I needed so many bulk items, I had to have a shopping cart and a flat cart. So my helper and I put one baby in the basket seat and the other two in the strollers. We took turns pushing the cart and the babies and dragging the flat cart.

As I was retrieving items up and down the aisles, the presence of three babies drew attention. It always does. On this Tuesday afternoon lots of people were stopping to see one baby, another baby, and then finally—you could see it register—a third baby. At that point, the question is usually, "Are they triplets?"

I'm quite accustomed to people saying, "Wow, you have your hands full!" "Boy, Girl, you have your hands full, don't you?" "Man, I bet you have your hands full." There are only so many ways you can say it. "Goodness, you have your hands full!"

What I haven't heard too many times is, "You poor thing!"

An older lady was standing next to my cart speaking to my helper when I arrived toting three large boxes of diapers. She looked my way and gave me her condolences. I could not believe she really said, "You poor thing!" Note to unthinking strangers: at some point young children will be able to understand what you are saying. Imagine if I'd had the three-year-old with us.

This time, I was ready. "Actually, we feel quite blessed," I said. I smiled, turned, and went down the next aisle. That was about as much conversation as she was going to get from me.

As my helper and I continued shopping, I said unkind things under my breath about a woman who gives condolences to you in public and calls you a "poor thing" because of your children. We both agreed that perhaps the woman was the one to be pitied. That comforted us, Survivors of Triplets. You may not like mountain climbing, Lady, but we find it extremely rewarding and character building and sometimes just sweet, like turning back as you're climbing down and saying, "That's an incredible view, People!"

We rounded the next aisle looking for bread, and another older woman stopped us.

"Oh my," she said. "Are these your precious babies? Why, they must be the most beautiful babies I've ever seen. Does the one in the cart have those same gorgeous blue eyes?"

"Yes, ma'am," I said, probably a bit too quickly. Aubrey turned on cue and looked at the lady. I gazed over the three and thought about how lucky I am, what sweet babies they are, and how glad I was that I'd hauled them out to shop. We were having an adventure.

The lady went on. "I need to get my husband to come see these beautiful children. Well, you are so blessed!" she said.

Later that day I mused about the two perspectives on my fruitfulness. The glass-half-full lady at the store told me that she, too, had three small children close in age, boys at that. She also remembered how people would see her busy little boys and say, "You've got your hands full!" That wise sister said she came up with a way to let people know not to pity her when they saw her busy family. She'd simply say, "Yeah, and so is my heart."

Sisters, whether you are piled high in Legos or girly tutus, you can still have unlikely moments of womanly grace at the big-box store. Thanks be to God.

Note

James Weldon Johnson, "The Creation," in *God's Trombones* (New York: Penguin Classics, 2008), 15.

CHAPTER 5

WHOEVER THE KIDS ARE, THEY ARE GOD'S

Then Philip opened his mouth, and beginning with this Scripture he told [the Ethiopian eunuch] the good news about Jesus. And as they were going along the road they came to some water, and the eunuch said, "See, here is water! What prevents me from being baptized?"
—*Acts 8:35-36 ESV*

The things that make me different are the things that make me.
—*Winnie the Pooh*

I started with a timpani drum, that huge kettle-looking percussion instrument. We had tickets to the symphony. Really good seats in the balcony. At the time, I was six months pregnant with Penn.

At one point during the concert—I have no memory of the exact piece of music—Rick, the percussionist, definitely had the rhythm going on the timpani. He was *ba-bamming* that big old drum with a fierceness that penetrates your whole body. In my expanded state, I could really feel the full-on percussion, but more compelling to me was the response coming from my baby boy. He was kicking it back in time to whatever he imagined was speaking to him: distant thunder, collapsing avalanches, or Mom's magnificent tummy rumbles.

It's probably a coincidence that the word *timpani* means "the hitting of one body against another." Or maybe the instrument was doing some crazy foreshadowing. We now live, for real, in a home where boys love to body slam one another. Often, I'm collateral damage. I had no idea that having four boys would mean that I am frequently hit in the face, my glasses knocked off, my head bumped, and my neck pulled; and, yes, as I try to calm violent situations, my voice is sometimes strained from yelling three rooms away. I turn on my historic Ronald Reagan voice, "Mr. Gorbachev, tear down that wall," or *don't* tear down that wall, because I need the little boys on the other side of it! Too bad there's no Fitbit to measure extreme mom endurance or how many daily calories we're burning from sheer physical child management and its related stress.

Back to the baby-timpani duet.

I wanted to make sure I wasn't imagining the *thump-thumping* because jacked-up hormones can make you think strange things. I took my husband's palm and placed it on my big belly. Victor's hand was somewhere on our baby boy, who was dancing around in there, pumping his feet, like tiny fists of triumph. We smiled. There was a guy in there who liked music or drums or dance or maybe all of it.

After Penn's in utero concert, he seemed to bounce into the world with a fixation on the church's drum kit. He had a toddler tendency to cut a musical rug, so we decided to give dance lessons a whirl. My husband is so *not* threatened by what people think, which is great; otherwise, he might have called the white coats on me a long time ago.

Our oldest son does dance and other musical stuff. These days he's working on some tiny piano compositions. When Penn fell in love with Satchmo, New Orleans, and the trumpet, we got him a starter trumpet for his birthday.

But the special class assignment is what really got to me. Penn built a set of chimes out of tall bamboo from a neighbor's yard and played *Ode to Joy* to demonstrate his instrument. That was one of those moments you realize your children will surpass you. I still think it began with the timpani, or that's when I took note. After all, he was kicking me. I think this love of music might be inside of him and part of who he is. I think it might be a gift.

Most Times, Sisters, Go with the Flow

Not wanting to label our kid or push him, we tried conformity in the form of T-ball. I'd assumed the boys would be involved in organized sports at some point, and lots of Penn's friends were signing up for a team. These moments are little boys' rites of passage, right? Besides, I'm rather romantic about baseball parks: I love sitting in webbed lawn chairs, having slow conversations, and eating concessions. People, I love the concessions! Baseball's so dang American. It also reminds me of my sweet stepdad, Pete, and the way he used to watch his favorite teams on TV with the A/C window unit blowing in the background on those extremely hot, southern summer days when you need gills simply to breathe.

I was sitting at one of Penn's four-year-old T-ball games on some rickety bleachers, not yet aware I could bring a lawn chair (which assumes you are organized). While watching those kiddos in all their cute clumsiness, I could see that some parents were so into baseball, or maybe so into their kid *in* baseball. This one little boy made an error (of course, they were all making errors); I

One of the grooviest things about Jesus is his openness to what's possible.

can't remember if he mis-hit the ball, ran to the wrong base, or dropped a ball. Who cared? It was supposed to be fun! As this bitty boy was coming near the dugout, his dad leaned in and said, "You can do better." I shot a look at the woman next to me, and she, too, seemed stunned.

I never want to be that guy. Actually, I didn't have to worry about the snarky baseball dad's mind-trip affecting my child, because after three seasons, Penn informed me that he had enough trophies and that the uniforms were idiotically hot. It was hard not to laugh. So long, baseball concessions. Guess we'll have to meet at the cold movie theater in the dark.

Maybe we needed a wetter sport, I thought. I'm a beach queen, and water is *so* my thing. Even the baptisms I perform as pastor are all messy and splashy. Wheee! Remember your baptism and be thankful—and drenched.

After summer swim lessons for a few years, Penn's coach—a tough, lovely woman known locally as the Swim Nazi—said he *had* to join a swim team. It was *his* sport, she insisted. Victor said, "Linda, you haven't seen him do ballet!"

It was true, though. Penn loved the water. It's such good exercise, so we signed him up for the big pool and real-live swim team. When I watched him, I marveled at his freestyle and breaststroke and how fast he picked it up. This was going to be his sport.

After a year, he asked to quit. He hated swimming laps. I asked him to finish the season, and it was one of the longest laps of my life. It was hard to let go of *my* dream, especially since he has a Michael Phelps body, but competitive swimming was not his thing. I asked his dad if we were being too soft. I mourned. I thought about a lost opportunity for a scholarship. But I also had a mother who, thankfully, told me she couldn't care less about my college major and more about my education, less about that one vocational thing people get hung up on and more about who I was becoming.

Our firstborn's tastes are not necessarily what I expected boydom to include, but he's not the only nonconformist in the house. No other boy has shown an interest in soccer or basketball or football. Two of our guys recently asked if they could learn weaving. They'd brought home school projects that were certainly nicer than the pot holders I made a trillion years ago. Score one for Mr. Baker, the art teacher. I'm seeing a pattern, especially after Aubrey insisted on cooking lessons with his Aunt Gayle. He is rather secretive, so maybe it has more to do with trying out cookie dough.

What finally proved we might not be mainstream was the boys' complete conversion to ice skating. It started with Wyatt, and then the other three fell, like dominoes, and I found myself freezing to death every Saturday morning for an hour and a half. You'd think that we knew Olympian ice skater Scott Hamilton or that we've got Nordic roots or that we live near tons of ice. OK, we *have* watched *Frozen* a lot.

It's OK if your boys like ice skating or dancing, and it's OK if your girls like building things and playing with trucks. Dang. I always wanted a slot car racetrack, so when my young nephew got one, I had to play with it. I fanatically wear cowboy boots, I don't ride horses regularly, and I don't live in a rural area. I also love football, action movies, and craft beer. I secretly want a tattoo, which means it's no longer a secret. I'm getting on up there, full-fledged midlife, so I've worried way too much about what my roomie at the nursing home will think.

However, life's awfully short. And God just loves creativity and diversity. So if we're dabbling in stuff that helps us grow and isn't dangerous, then it's probably OK to see where the train is headed.

Not So Vanilla, Mom

There's a great promotional video of Idris Elba, the British actor, asking adults what they want to be when they grow up. When he poses the question, there's lots of nervous laughter. But Elba gently reminds each adult, "You do realize that you're still growing, right?" After chewing on that, people begin to share dreams: make quilts, be a football coach, play drums, act, pilot a hot air balloon. When asked why they haven't pursued the dream, most say time is running out.

That may be accurate, but what's also happened is that adults forget how glorious the world we live in actually is. Children, however, are in the thick of it, seeing life for the first time. They haven't learned to tame their dreams or say no to possibilities. And if they are very fortunate, they haven't absorbed the insidious assumption that they are and must be like everyone else.

And this is where I find Jesus to be very groovy. (I hope you still like me, but yes, I sometimes say *groovy*.)

One of the grooviest things about Jesus is his openness to what's possible: new life, change, growth, breathing fresh air, breaking some molds. When you read stories about Jesus, you begin to see patterns that a lot of people find alarming. He's simply not your run-of-the-mill, vanilla Messiah.

Let's be honest. Jesus hung out with anybody, like *anybody*. It didn't matter if they had money or health or a good reputation or were less than marginally religious. It didn't matter if the people he visited scammed the poor, had a different worship style, were divorced, were the wrong ethnicity or gender or age, or basically were all-out unclean according to the prescribed rules of his own religious tradition. Jesus would literally eat with anyone, and it got him in trouble with certain religious authorities, and it might get us in trouble. I'm pretty sure that Jesus would get some haters on Facebook with all his jazzed-up coloring outside the lines: "You have heard it said, but I say…." Picture the opposition leaning in, heads shaking, tut-tutting, "Really, Jesus! Who do you think you are?"

I love Jesus precisely because his ministry startles our comfortable, settled lives. Jesus's ministry is like the arched rainbow that the boys and I saw as a rain shower passed through one afternoon. We saw the entire rainbow, end to end. It's fascinating to consider that the rainbow occurs because the light hits the front of a water droplet, bends upon entering, then bounces off the back of the droplet and heads back toward us, transformed. Plain old regular white light is actually rainbow sherbet.

Jesus's love is light that bends toward way more dreams, beauty, diversity, and possibility than I ever could alone.

I have a particular image of Jesus in my mind. As Jesus encounters all these exotic people and ministers to them, he says to himself, "That Sister just blows my mind. That Sister is an original. Oh wow, that Brother, wow, he's so unique." Jesus notices and embraces the colorful difference and uniqueness of creation, all that God said was and is good, which makes us very fortunate because we are part of the good stuff, whoever we are. That is also good news for our kids.

One of my favorite stories about Jesus is a real family bombshell and, frankly, a real turnoff if you like to have the inside track and are more comfortable with vanilla. Three of the Gospels tell a version of this awkward incident, but I think Mark's version is the most intense.

Jesus has been going about his ministry, hanging out and healing all the wrong people at all the wrong times. It's even gotten back to his family. Thinking he's lost it, his mother and brother and sisters go to retrieve him: "When his family heard what was happening, they came to take control of him. They were saying, 'He's out of his mind!'" (Mark 3:21).

We're not going to find joy or authenticity or contentment when we constantly look for the next big thing.

Do you have the type of family who would try to keep you quiet on occasions? I share way too much for my own good and others' comfort. The older I get, the worse it gets. I almost bought a shirt that read, "Don't hate me because I look this good at fifty-five." My brother, Steve, keeps me in check: "TMI, Sis. TMI." Secretly, I like to push it so he'll rein me in. All of us kids need to know that someone's watching, that someone cares enough to make sure we don't totally fall off the edge.

Let's consider why Jesus's family is upset. The Gospel story says they want control of Jesus, which strikes me as a real live stuff-hitting-the-fan situation. Because, obviously, Jesus practices unconditional, unlimited love, they think he's going too far, even for his family, and they know what's best, right? Sometimes, your family means well when they meddle. After all, the people who raised you usually know you better than anyone. Maybe Jesus's family was afraid for him or their reputation or his reputation or that he would trash his future or have regrets about the night he ate with that *[whisper]* adulterous woman. I feel for the family. What Jesus was doing was not what everyone else was doing, and who knows where that would lead?

That happened once or twice in my immediate family—that not doing what everyone else is expected to do.

My oldest brother, the patriarch of our family these days, went to seminary way before I, the baby, did. Jack left home to become a pastor and studied at Southern Methodist University in the mid-1960s, at a time of great social unrest. While there, he became involved in the civil rights movement.

When the national evening news began reporting about the violence taking place in Selma, Alabama, Mom phoned Jack's dorm. His roommate answered and told her that her son was not there. She demanded to know if he'd gone to Selma. He had.

My parents got in the car and drove down to Dallas to meet with the dean of Perkins School of Theology and some other professors. The meeting was cordial, but my parents wanted to know exactly why their son's seminary was teaching him to get involved in dangerous and deadly activities.

No dummy, Mom had read a lot of the works of biggie Protestant theologians, including Dietrich Bonhoeffer's *The Cost of Discipleship*.

As my parents and the professors discussed the implications of following a Lord who promised liberation of the oppressed, my mom began to better understand the reasons the seminary had encouraged the students to be involved.

"But," Mom finally said in the meeting, "if this cause is as central to discipleship as you say, then why aren't there any professors going to march with the students?"

Boom.

Faculty representatives from the Perkins School of Theology were on the next bus to Selma.

God's limitless love is scary. If we let our kids open up their tender, unspoiled hearts to the world, anything can happen. Yet people who faithfully follow a divine dissident like Jesus can't be all sweet and no spice. Sisters, there has to be some hot sauce.

Less Comparing, Please

Not long ago, I was having coffee with a new mom who is also enjoying the experience of triplet babies. She's doing great. Remarkable, I think. As we visited, she mentioned that one of her babies sleeps a lot. Fantastic! She wondered aloud if too much tummy time had lessened this baby's progress in lifting her head. The other two seemed to be further along.

That's how it begins. We worry endlessly about our children and where they are on the pediatric growth chart and countless other ways to classify. Americans are preoccupied with every sort of bracket. (That's why it's called March Madness, all that crazy guessing about who's best.) Ranking is one of our truly neurotic national pastimes.

I get that it's hard not to compare people in the same family, especially for those who have more than one child or who are surrounded by obnoxious people who are habitually measuring. Even if parents manage to avoid it, comparisons, real or imagined, erupt amongst individual children. And believe you me, they will remind you every day what you did for someone else instead of them. My boys love to tell me how unfair I am. When the report cards come home, I pray the grades are all the same, but, of course, they are not. So I pray they are pretty close. *It's OK! I love you too, Woody. You don't have to push Buzz out the window.*

It's probably no accident that coveting is listed as a top-ten sin. It's the ultimate comparing of who you are and what you have and then believing contentment is found outside your unique you. Wanting what other people have—even a more "normal" life, whatever that is— can drive you cuckoo because fixation on what we think we want or need, as well as frequent comparisons with that person's life over there, sucks the joy right out of life.

I'm going to put some of the blame on Pinterest, Zillow, and Houzz, the apps on my phone that equip me to compare my house, closet, kitchen, porch, and, therefore, my life to someone else's. If I spend too much time in the company of my helpful apps contemplating upgrades, I will believe that everyone else has a better home, kids, and pocketbook than I have.

One of my favorite home-decorating books is by a woman who says perfection is overrated. This sister actually believes there's beauty in the lived-in and loved-on and just about used-up. We're not going to find joy or authenticity or contentment when we constantly look for the next big thing.

There's a great story about how Jesus was confronted by a woman, actually a momma, who invites him not to give all the attention to the firstborn (see Matthew 15:21-28; Mark 7:24-29). Spunky, huh? She comes from a Gentile area near Tyre and Sidon. In other words, she's not Jewish. And yet, as Jesus escapes with his disciples for a little rest by the beach, this woman finds them, talks their ears off, and will not—I mean, will not—shut up.

This outsider momma has come to Jesus for her daughter. The girl is having some problems, some demons, she says. Who knows what they are? Stuff parents worry about. Anorexia, bullying, Snapchat. She's not leaving without some help for her child. After all, she's someone's mother. Jesus used a cute little children's illustration to tell her that his priority is Israel, the first child, but she pushes Jesus with a snappy comeback. He said, "'The children have to be fed first. It isn't right to take the children's bread and toss it to the dogs.' But she answered, 'Lord, even the dogs under the table eat the children's crumbs'" (Mark 7:28).

Touché, Sister! Teachable moment!

I think Jesus had to admire her zinger response. I know I do. Besides, it seems fairly Rabbi worthy, right? Ultimately, the story doesn't give us every detail of this cool encounter, but I like to think the woman's challenge encouraged Jesus to go even further in his boundary-breaking ministry. *Take the three-pointer, Lord!* She may not be from the house of Israel, but she's gonna call on the Son of David because, I think, she gets it. Jesus can cross over and make the family bigger. That's really reaching people who may be beyond your comfort zone. Jesus is always going across, through, and beyond the predictable range of grace, where comparisons collapse into a heap of unconditional love. I'll take those crumbs any day.

Let Your Freak Flag Fly

I live in Little Rock, Arkansas, home of Central High School. It is a key site of a major event in the American civil rights movement. The group called the Little Rock Nine are the African American students who in 1957 helped carry out the *Brown v. Board of Education* Supreme

Court mandate to integrate all schools "with all deliberate speed." It was not smooth at all, and the students faced horrendous discrimination and harassment. What happened was unspeakable, but we have to speak so that we don't forget.

Paul McCartney gave a concert in Little Rock and got to meet two of the Little Rock Nine. Along with John Lennon, McCartney wrote the song "Blackbird," specifically hoping it would encourage those living in the midst of the volatile march for desegregation and civil rights.

> Blackbird singing in the dead of night;
> Take these broken wings and learn to fly;

One of the most important ways I know to help my kids be all God intends is to go against the herd when that herd attempts to hurt or harm other humans. In my tradition, we confess that God inhabited the skin of a Jewish homeless peasant, whose wings we broke. (We humans are good at mishandling one another.) Yet out of that brokenness God offered a new day and new relationships, even a new family, a colorful, rainbow family.

Jesus crosses over and unites us, but we're tasked with sharing that good news. That's why I intentionally swim upstream, looking for diverse friends in a divided world. It's called "witness," and I suppose sometimes others may think I'm a freak; but I think I'm on the really colorful Jesus squad. I must be doing something right because my oldest was devastated when his two dearest friends in school were in different classes this year. And he's the minority friend with his white skin and blond hair, which he wishes would stand up tall and proud like his friend's frohawk.

Difference is everywhere. I look in our freezer to see what ice cream flavors are there: the Great Divide (chocolate and vanilla), chocolate chip cookie dough, mint chocolate chip, pistachio almond, and, occasionally, cherry vanilla. And there are also the various frozen creations at least thirty days old that some little boy concocted to see how glaciers erode. How about that? All different.

CHAPTER 6

SELFIE

Love your neighbor as yourself.
—Luke 10:27

We have all a better guide in ourselves, if we would attend to it, than any
other person can be.
—Jane Austen

Confession: I sometimes refuse to shower and get cleaned up on the grounds that, even when I have the time, it's rebellious to run errands without any makeup, with hair in a clip, and wearing sweaty gym clothes. Scrumptiously self-indulgent.

In my big, small town, it's nice to go unnoticed at the hardware store or the post office because sometimes I just want to be alone. Yep, I love those hotspots, the smell of metal and the good old days of stamps. Before Penn's week-long church-camp experience all by himself, I had to explain the concept of stamps to him and the reality that we wouldn't be communicating for four days—except for the miracle of mail—like, from the mailbox.

Honestly, not getting dressed to go out is one of my off-grid strategies. While I love people, and I'm always running into people, I don't always want to talk about *anything*. I don't want to talk about how my family is, which is hard to avoid. Oh, and my husband was in politics. And there's that thing about me: I am a pastor, and I have been to a lot of church potlucks and functions. Believe it or not, sometimes I don't even want to talk about the church or why suffering exists if God is all loving. I have my limits. Do you see these sunglasses? They are my version of being a Jesuit. Sometimes I simply want to concentrate fully on getting my toes done and tackle powering up the rolling balls in the salon massage chair.

Actually, it's a luxury to choose not to shower. When the boys were tiny, I didn't always get a regular shower. I wanted one—a good long one—but it wasn't always possible. I was more concerned about other people's hygiene. Truly, I obsessed over it. It was self-preservation of the most primitive kind. Germ warfare.

When the triplets came home, I put carafes of hand sanitizer in every place human eyes might spot them. With four little ones, I thought I needed squirtable pure alcohol or something pretty close, to avoid illnesses that might spread throughout the entire household. What would happen if everyone got sick? The ship and the captain might go down. That was a nutty notion, but, in those days, I could not mentally survive if I considered contagion beyond a certain level. So I lovingly said to everyone who crossed our home's threshold, "Did you see the hand sanitizer? Right there? See it?" I'm sure they were on to my rigid, desperate, take-some-prisoners message and strained smile. God bless those helpers who came and went, but they weren't actually living with the little germ vectors, were they? For heaven's sake, they could go home.

Early on in mother land, with four small babies, I was in survival mode, like the way I didn't want to get sick and tried to control germs. I think a lot of moms feel as if they are hanging on. *Can I stand up? Can I walk? Can I change diapers?* Perhaps obsessing about hand sanitizer demonstrated that I set my own bar of self-care a tad too low. Oh, well. Exhaustion explains a lot of mental and emotional misfires.

One evening, tornadoes were swirling around our house because we live in a place that apparently creates and likes that kind of excitement. Victor was in DC. My middle brother, Tom, came by to stay and keep watch as the storms passed through, just in case we needed to evacuate all four children to a safer place in the house.

I was fortunate to have Nanny Rho, our tinies' helper, spending the night with us. Penn's sitter, before the triplets were born, dropped by because my oldest had a horrible stomach bug and had to be put in the bath almost every hour to get clean again. I was desperately trying to keep everyone separate because I was still pumping my milk and breast-feeding. At one point, little Penn's lower abdomen rumbled mercilessly. We all heard it, then silence. Finally, Tom said, "Whoa, *The China Syndrome*," referencing the old movie about a nuclear meltdown. Tornadoes, triplets, and thunder down under.

The Quest for Selfie

Having children is not only a life adjustment but also a whole new way to learn what it means to be self-concerned and self-interested. Because we're women, we may have the idea that we're created for self-sacrifice, giving up big swaths of ourselves for the betterment of the people in our lives, whether spouse, kids, family, friends, or work. My spiritual tradition hasn't taught me to believe God created me, a woman, only for others, but some Christians suggest as much. I disagree, choosing to believe God delights in creativity and love more than utility. Even so, too often, I've bought into the idea that I'm more useful than lovable.

Here's a familiar example. Predictably, I get energized by a project in my home or at work, and the next thing you know, I'm overdoing it, driven to see something completed, done, finished. While signaling strength on the outside, strength I don't always feel, I send myself to the end of the line, depleted. Of course there are loads of times I am glad to give to others with love when it's needed or even wanted, but giving until there's little left of yourself is discounting God's own creation—you—and taking off your own oxygen mask.

I'm so glad God created therapists and healers. Through them, I am slowly and steadily learning that if a plane loses altitude and you have idiotically placed your child's oxygen mask on before your own, that may be the last thing you ever do for your child or anyone else.

I've seen oxygen masks. Not attractive. Not comfortable. They are definitely not trending as a fashion accessory. Although I'm more comfortable wearing one these days, that doesn't mean I don't get busy doing things that aren't really necessary. Metaphorically, I often cram my mask in the depths of my closet, under my 1984 Madonna tapestry jeans, where I forget about it and no one knows to ask me if I'm still breathing because I can wave and smile. On my deathbed, I'll probably be waving and smiling. There are times when, like a lot of women, I don't want anyone to see me needing to breathe, which is totally unspiritual and unloving toward myself and a really stinky example of Christian living. We think we don't look good in oxygen masks, and we certainly have a hard time admitting they help us. But we do need to breathe, even if it's just so inconvenient.

I've seen Kim Kardashian in all her glory. In fact, most of us have seen Kim and her sisters in all their glory. When Kim Kardashian Tweets her bum, it's just so full of *herself*. Certainly, I want all of us women to be proud of our bodies, every kind of body, and to care for our bodies. So here's to Kim and her busy buns that look good. But we also need to ask Kim to scoot over so that we can love on all types: sturdy, delicate, and in-between. I don't mean we should celebrate exclusively a variety of female body types, but rather a way of being fully who we're meant to be, who God calls us to be, not only as spouse, mom, sister, and daughter, but as ourselves, completely.

When I was a lot younger and more sensitive, I was married to someone who told me my ideal weight was 115 pounds. Because I wanted to keep his love and please him, I let him define me for a season, but it turned out to be a vicious cycle. I came too close to developing an eating disorder because I thought way too much about how much I ate, or didn't, rather than being healthy. If we live by the judgments and expectations of others, we may begin to chop off a part of the self, then another part until, well, there's not much left. When we're willing or allowed to share only our presentable selves, rather than our trippy selves, our excruciatingly vulnerable selves, our quivering-mass-of-doubts self, as well as our obvious victorious self, we're not living fully, wholly, or faithfully.

What we need to do is practice valuing who we are becoming at each stage of life.

Sisters, you've probably guessed that I've not yet graduated summa cum laude from the school of self-care, but I have some ideas about what self-care is and what it's not. No matter who you are, you need "selfie hygiene," and I'm not talking about a quick fix found on a pop-up ad. We don't need any more suggestions about what to wear past thirty and how to apply makeup past fifty. Can we please just pause that stuff? And, my sweet Sisters, those harmful, external messages that bombard us are yet another reason why we need to practice crafting our very own selfies. We live in a way crazy-pants world, but we can learn to craft self-care that matters and sustains us.

Jesus as a Study in Selfie

I remember the first time I saw a long stick with a phone attached to the end of it. We had taken the boys to Disney World, a first trip to the Magic Kingdom. I watched as people pulled out their selfie sticks and captured scenic landscapes of Cinderella's castle with themselves in the foreground. I learned that my camera had a broken lens the first day at the park. I was really annoyed with myself for not checking out my camera before the trip. I was annoyed that Victor is not "in charge" of my camera. And I was annoyed that I had no idea about selfie sticks. I failed in setting up the best way to capture the memories, which meant I was judging myself, feeling guilty, and struggling with unrealistic expectations for a working mother of four. Ruminating about taking quality pictures was not going to get me in the moment.

Jesus was so good in the moment. He was almost always really *with* people. As you read along in the Gospels, it's fairly clear Jesus was specifically tending people, teaching them, correcting them, eating with them, loving them—you know—like a parent. He pays such close attention to who we are and what our needs truly are.

Every day, then, Jesus was available to folks. But that's also why he sought retreat and quiet, either in the mountains, on the other side of the lake, or at a good friend's home where he could chill out and eat some home cooking. I can't see Jesus ever saying, "No thanks," to Martha's mac and cheese. That's so rude and not in the moment or caring for self. I can't remember ever reading a Bible story, not one, about Jesus saying anything like, "Can't sit and talk. Can't stay. I'm just too busy." It's true that he was busy, and sometimes he was even delayed in getting to his next stop, but mostly he let encounters unfold. It doesn't mean he didn't ask pointed questions about who we're called to be, but Jesus lingered and helped others get comfortable in their own skins, love themselves, and put themselves in the picture.

When we were at Disney World, my husband ate ice cream nonstop. OK, a lot. This tallish, health-conscious, attractive man ate Mickey Mouse ears (vanilla ice cream shaped like Mickey and dipped in chocolate) every day. About two in the afternoon, we had to locate a food cart in Disney World and take a Mickey Mouse ice-cream break for Daddy. While I loved being with my children at this ridiculously commercial playground, there was nothing like seeing my husband thoroughly enjoying nibbling Mickey's ears away every day. I'm not sure I got any pictures of Victor and his ice-cream habit, but I'll never forget it, because I was there, fully. It's one of my sweetest memories, that and watching Aubrey raise his hand to fight the evil Darth Vader, whom he fearlessly defeated during a light saber duel.

Being Just You and Nothing Else

One day I was shopping at a drug store, picking up a few items for my trip to Israel, when I discovered a product I'd never seen, probably because I hate to go to the store.

If I have to go to a store, I'd much rather go to flea markets and thrift stores because you can redeem stuff, like the old end tables I got for our little cabin. You can find something magical at places that fool you by smelling musty and old. But older isn't all bad. Older can mean a rich and luscious experience. If you're young, please write that down and don't forget it, because women in our culture think they are supposed to be physically beautiful all the time, forever, which misses more than the eye can see. What we need to do is practice valuing who we are becoming at each stage of life.

What I found at the drugstore that day was something called a wrinkle releaser. I picked up a small bottle and threw it in my cart, never imagining that it would iron my clothes all by itself after just a few strategic squirts. To make me feel like I was really working, while on the trip, I took time to hang the article of clothing up near the shower and shoot it with some more positron rays, and voila! I didn't look like I'd slept in my clothes. On the bus, I mentioned my discovery of this miracle product to a younger clergy friend, and she said the product saved her loads of time in college. I wondered how many hours I'd spent ironing in college back in the day and decided any ironing is probably too much. I love the smell of starch and the steam, but that's about it. I'm glad you younger women have got this.

I have one bestie in the world who can make me laugh until I cry and cross my legs. It's my sister—my lovely sister—who went to Israel with me. Gayle is nineteen years older than I am. And even though we weren't raised in the same era, we are blessed to think highly of each other and talk almost every day, sometimes more than once a day. We go through the checklist of how our children are doing—including her grown ones—recipes, people we don't understand, politics, the church, and our spiritual connection to Jesus.

> *I wondered how many hours I'd spent ironing in college and decided any ironing is probably too much.*

That's why, when I finally decided I wanted to go to the Holy Land, I knew it had to be with my sister. At first, Sister was worried about the walking since she's now in her seventies. Next, she was worried about security. Those are understandable concerns. It's amazing to say that she worries because she's my number one go-to person to tell me not to worry. She usually worries small-scale, like where are we going to lunch and how do we get there? After all, she's got perspective, having seen it all.

I'm still in the stage of worrying about the big stuff, like whether I am a decent mother, wife, and pastor. Or I'll ask her if she thinks I have too much of the confrontational gene, like one of our aunts who used to threaten, "Do you want me to unscrew your naval, take off your legs, and beat your brains out?"

Yes, this was a scary threat, but I loved our Aunt Toodles (yes, that is what we called my flamboyant aunt) because she was sharp and funny, with hair always perfectly done, thin and dressed to the nines all her life, who worked, smoked in a sexy way, drank cocktails, played cards, and introduced me to nachos and Blue Bell ice cream. Mom didn't drink much at all, but let me tell y'all, she did buy some Coco Lopez when she got home from Toodles's because, for the first time in her life, Mom had tasted a piña colada.

Sometime after we got home from the Holy Land pilgrimage, Sullivan was spraying the wrinkle releaser around recklessly in our bathroom (because children are always in your bathroom). I asked him not to waste Precious. As he was spraying what could have been a toxic yard spray, Sullivan wanted to know what it was, and I told him. My child said, "Oh, you spray it on your face!" How had I not thought of that myself? I immediately called my sister and told her this revelation given by one of my kids. I had to sit down and cross my legs as we laughed together.

This is some of my medicine.

Sister knew me before I was Momma. She not only helped raise me and is my second mom, but she also knows all the crap, inside and out, and she knows the greatest stuff too. Almost all of us have people in our lives who knew us before we were Mom, and we need not live in the past, but we can cherish the roots we share with our besties.

The Great Escape Is Up to You

When our kids were really little, there were few days that I had any time to myself. Back then, I actually did enjoy shopping, but only because I was out of the house for an activity. I couldn't really count those chores as Sabbath to discover who I was, separate from all these other roles of mom, wife, and pastor. It's like saying that I enjoyed Diaper Fun, our local kids-only movement class, or Kindermusik, the early music appreciation course for toddlers with tambourines and bells and loud things. Of course, I celebrated the activities as times to be with my children and dip into their development, but that didn't help me sort out me.

I've already mentioned my love of pedicures, which is a nice mini escape, but sometimes we need to block out time on our calendars for being with self. We all have to decide what takes care of us.

My friend, Gayle, who worked with me at one of my churches, taught me that I needed to decompress after church funerals. Before that, I had often gone immediately back to the church and tried to work. Sometimes we can't avoid certain obligations, but after Gayle's modeling, I saw that I needed to block time out for myself after a very emotionally draining experience, which included preparing the service, caring for the family, and actually doing the service with very personal words and actions of care.

Nowadays, I always take the rest of the day off after a funeral to decompress. In fact, Gayle and I have used the time after the service for retail therapy, sometimes buying locally made granola, stopping in a shop off the beaten path, or even purchasing a pair of boots in another county. It wasn't the purchases but the experience of retreat that came from the enjoyment of the senses and the realization of being alive.

As our boys grew physically, we began to rent cabins around the state, hiking and fishing and playing more in nature. I was also renting places several times a year to write and plan and reflect. My husband and I decided to look for our own cabin and were fortunate enough to find an affordable place near some caves, trails, and fishing streams. While we love it as a family, I also use it by myself for quiet and to listen to God. It's still hard for me to leave my family, but I know that cultivating time for me will help me and show my kids how to love themselves and listen to themselves better. I also hope that someday in the future they will give the women in their lives permission to do the same.

Some of us feel most alive in nature, so we need to block off time for walking, hiking, fishing, or whatever it is that helps us grab hold of us as a singular child of God and reminds us there is no other one like us. The great Catholic thinker, paleontologist, and naturalist Pierre Teilhard de Chardin, who is one of my mom's favorites, said, "There is a communion with God and a communion with earth, and a communion with God through the earth." (These Jesuits are the real deal.) So ask yourself, "What is my particular escape, and when am I going to take it?"

Have a Little Compassion

There are some ways we women and moms need to work the compassion thing harder. You probably know that *compassion* means "suffering with." Clearly, it's in the DNA of Christianity, since Jesus often demonstrated compassion, most especially to those who felt helpless and harassed (see Matthew 9:36), who were like lost sheep (see Mark 6:34), who were hungry (see Mark 8:2), who needed healing (see Matthew 14:14; Matthew 20:34; and Mark 1:40-41), or who were bereaved (Luke 7:12-18). The many needs of others moved Jesus to provide, but he also refreshed himself and had compassion for himself, letting others anoint him with oil and feed him from their tables, which meant he knew how to receive.

We women are so hard on one another and ourselves. We talk about one another, our clothes, our sizes, our homes, and our kids and their achievements or stumbles. If we don't have compassion for ourselves, we can't have compassion for others, a hallmark of those who follow Jesus.

All of the churches I've served have offered animal-blessing services near the Feast of St. Francis of Assisi, the Catholic Church's patron saint of animals and the environment. A few years ago, the church I served sponsored a service and an adoption day by the local humane society. One of the dogs, a small rat-terrier-looking guy, was shivering. It wasn't that cold, and he was obviously scared. When we learned his story—how he was skin and bones when they found him, had survived distemper, and had lost some vision—we understood his fear. Aubrey, who loves every creature, big and small, concerned the pup was cold, removed his shirt as the sun was setting on a first Sunday in October and put it around the dog. My child gave a homeless dog the shirt off his back. You know how this story ends, right? Of course the dog came home with us.

We need compassion like that for ourselves, whether we've lost it with our kids—and we all do at some point—whether we're uncertain about the next phase of life, when we're confused about what our future goals ought to be, and most especially when we clearly believe we've failed.

Right now, most of my goals are getting easier.

1. Please, someone, let me inherit a tiny house. I love those compact living spaces. They are dollhouse cute and would inspire me to get rid of more stuff that will never help me love myself better.

2. Never run out of hand soap. I don't use the antibacterial harsh stuff anymore. I learned that the 99 percent germ-free stuff is creating superbugs, so I go for the nonabrasive, delicious basil, rhubarb, or

lemon verbena varieties. The soap's not merely for making me clean or for protecting others and the environment; it's for taking care of me. Almost every time I smell that great soap seeping up from my clean hands, I'm reminded of how God wants me to let go of the dirt I'm hanging on to and just be the best selfie I'm supposed to be.

CHAPTER 7

THE SKINIFICATION OF
DIVINE LOVE

Treat people in the same way that you want them to treat you.
—Luke 6:31

Love your curves and all your edges;
All your perfect imperfections.
—"All of Me," John Legend

Jesus may not have been married, but he had family. As far as we can tell, he was raised by two loving, yet human parents *and* had siblings (see Matthew 12:46-50). The natural order of things is to attack your siblings. No wonder Jesus got the thankless job of peacemaker.

Jesus's family was not merely biological, though. He made it clear that we all belong to God first. We are children of God and therefore related and actual kinfolk whether we are widows, outcasts, children, poor fishermen, sick and suffering, or of various religious traditions, beliefs, and ethnicities. Jesus, who had been a refugee and was an itinerant rabbi, lived as one who didn't own a home but, because of love, had a family.

It's our story, and God is in our story, and each day we choose each other all over again.

That doesn't mean Jesus's family got along all the time. Jesus and his closest followers lived and worked side by side with one another daily. At times, he was clearly (heavy sigh) frustrated with their limited view of family, but Jesus never quit trying to create and strengthen God's family, even as he was dying (see John 4:1-42; 13:1-18; and 19:25-29). After Jesus's ascension, his followers scattered, paralyzed by grief and fear, but he called them to come together in unity (see Acts 1:1-14). Jesus wouldn't give up on bringing together all the people who make up God's family.

Life in a community with other weirdo human beings will always be challenging and sometimes—maybe most times—extremely frustrating.

Why?

It's all in the Jesus story, or the story of God in human skin.

Jesus's story looks a lot like the story of our families. Some of Jesus's family was worried about waste and priorities (see Mark 14:4-5). Someone else complained about having to feed everyone who showed up, even when there was hardly enough for a few disciples (see Matthew 14:15-16). Another one thought they shouldn't let the children come along (see Matthew 19:13-14). Another's in-law butted in and demanded her kids should be treated better than the rest (see Matthew 20:20-22). And you can be sure there was always one who was worried about paying the taxes on time (see Matthew 9:9-10).

Do any of us really believe that Jesus's life in community with limited, finite, and sinful humans wasn't a good test case in how to learn to love our families, spouses included?

We're not Jesus, but there are ways we can look to his style and habit of loving and forgiving. And I bet the best way to learn about Jesus's love is by practicing that love most faithfully on the person next to us in the king-size bed.

Two Sides of the Same Coin

I often ask God, "Can Victor and I be any different?" And when I ask this question, it's not rhetorical. It's a prayer. I'm really asking God if God's noticed. And I really want God to say something like, "Well, Honey, no, you two can't be any different. I've noticed that too."

If God answered obligingly, I could go down my mental list of differences. We all have that list.

ONE SIDE

Victor doesn't think the boys need to shampoo their hair or wash bodies after swimming—for five days in a row.

He's terrible at directions but always wants to drive and always asks the same questions about where to turn.

He always buys the off-brand stuff. I hate his paper towels.

He has an entire locker in which to put his stuff, but it's full so he puts his wallet on top of the china cabinet. I am totally petrified of his closet and what's hiding in there.

He worries about the boys' safety (we still don't have the bunk beds we need), but he doesn't get movie ratings at all and needs guidance.

He never whines about illness and went septic. He should be weaker and complain more, like me.

He doesn't get the concept of separating laundry or that we have lots of bins of laundry in *all* our bedrooms.

He doesn't grasp change at all (he has flannel shirts older than I am), and I fear we will never move. I'm worried the kids will be stuck with cleaning out our junk after they've hauled us out.

He's cheap. I don't like his really harsh, destroy-my-color-job shampoo. I think I mentioned the paper towels.

You can tell his late-night snack was an orange by the peelings on the coffee table next to his chair. I love it when he goes all crazy and eats ice cream.

"So that's one side," I say.

"Are you through?" God asks.

"Sort of."

"We could sit here complaining all day long, and that isn't going to change a thing, Darlin'! You picked him, both of you with all your contrariness, as family. You picked him to teach you all about the real you. You picked him to teach you what love means. You also picked him to teach you about me."

I sigh and say, "Oh God, pleeeeease!"

And God says, "That's OK! Let it out, Sweet One, go on and let it all out! Big deep breaths."

I feel really vulnerable, then, because I know God is absolutely right. And then I'm sad because we won't get fifty years.

THEN THE OTHER SIDE

Victor is a very good father, better than ours were by a long shot, and likely as stressed as I am because parenting is exhausting.

He's so cheap, and that's why we have money, which is a good thing for a Singleton because we'd be on the dole, the way Irish author Frankie McCourt described his struggling family's charitable assistance from the Society of St. Vincent de Paul.

He recycles, which includes wearing clothes from 1972. I think I mentioned that already. (Dirty little secret: I've sneaked some of his older ties out of the house and off to Goodwill.)

He's very generous.

He insists on doing his own yard work. I've learned that he can create a thing of beauty with rocks and plants, even if our yard does always need to be mowed in the summer because he's too busy building gardens to cut the grass!

He loves animals and carries Penn's cat on his shoulders like a sack of potatoes to put in our big boy's room for the night. That makes me smile before bedtime.

He will go see any movie I want to see, even chick flicks and action and Disney movies. He actually loves theater. You never know about former Marines.

He goes along with my love of the beach.

He has rarely ever missed a sermon I've preached and has always supported me as a pastor. Once he wrote a wonderful Christmas hymn for the church I served.

He gave me my children, and no matter how many nasty science experiments I find in the freezer made by sweet little boy hands, I will always love him for helping me get them here.

"See there," says God slyly, "it takes both sides to make the glorious whole, both the in sync and the distinct contrast."

Lord knows, I have my own two sides, including Sweet Sass and Sister Sinister.

I'm sure my desire to change everything every five minutes is about the most upsetting reality in Victor's world. I'm impatient and creative, and my tail sometimes wags faster than a dog's. I'm bright red Hot Tamales in a box. I'm an annoying bee in bright yellow and black stripes. I laugh too loud, slap my knee, and use strong language when I get a strong whiff of phony, narcissism, or a snob job. And then there's the sad-sack-clown me from *Toy Story 3*, Chuckles, who crashes hard and goes monotone. Sometimes you just have to let the clown go all boo-hoo with a time-out and the reassurance you will be there when she (or he) is ready. Victor mostly gets all that spicy, but exhausting me, both sides of the same coin. And I mostly get him. Together, we're creating something new. It's our story, and God is in our story, and each day we choose each other all over again. That's what all couples must do to grow. It's some of the deepest and hard spiritual work you will ever do.

Maybe, some days, we both need to let the dishes stay in the sink longer.

The Oversplaining

Men are wonderful. I love them, but they tend to overexplain stuff or problem solve, even to the point of assuming that we women want them to solve our problems when most times we just need emotional support. I've read that even one hour a week listening to and observing your child engaged in some activity, whether reading or sports, provides the gift of presence. Simply paying attention is sacred time.

Me: "I'm not sure what I should do about [describe issue that is usually upsetting, frustrating, or causing anger]."

My Man: "Well, it seems to me you have these specific options. Number one..."

Me: "OK, so I know all that, but I want you to hug me and tell me it will be OK and that I'm wonderful, beautiful, and confidant and this situation is intolerable. I want to know you will go fight them like Jon Snow in *Game of Thrones* if they defame my honor and integrity. Actually, I want you to listen to me as I tell you the whole ball of wax."

So here's to mysplaining:

We all need to be heard, women and men, so listen. Just listen. Maybe practice.

We're all responsible for taking care of our own needs.

We're all insecure and idiosyncratic, but it's still our responsibility to communicate what we want without resentment or the bizarre expectation that the other person knows what we're thinking through some Vulcan mind-meld. (I agree that's cool, but it's not real.)

We all should quit composing in our heads the list of what the spouse has done for us lately, or not.

We need to realize that marriage is a deal that can't be measured by an equal division of labor every day. It's called "More grace, please."

We might want to let the guys do it their way, and we can do it ours.

My sweet husband has no idea why I replaced our china cabinet with a drink station, and I cannot understand why he won't sell the old 1996 truck that sits in front of our house and doesn't run unless you give it a jump. Not even Viagra can help that truck, Honey.

Maybe, some days, we both need to let the dishes stay in the sink longer, not as a test to see who'll do them first, but as a pact we make together to set some limits on all that stuff to which we are giving way too much of our energy. Go rogue and stop, rest, and Sabbath more.

A Night on the Town, Also Known As: Spending Time Without the Kids

We have a fairly large fenced-in backyard for our three dogs. But we still have a lot of canine lounging on my pillows and sofas, with accompanying shed phenomena.

The adopted Pointer, Nori, loves to hunt, especially at night, but only when it's warm. Understand that she's cold natured. I wonder if this is the reason the hunting life didn't work out for her. She's totally thrilled to come when we call, as long as the temp is low and all creatures great and small are hibernating. But don't bother her when spring has sprung, unless she's caught something she wants to lay at your feet. Then, well, she's all smiles and wags and mission accomplished.

Dogs are not the only ones who like a night out on the town. All married people need them. Victor and I have always tried to keep a standing Saturday date night, even when the boys pulled on my leg and sobbed and cried "Mooommmaaa" as we walked out the door. (I know it's hard to believe, but they turn off the tears as soon as the car is out of view.) Do all you can to make and keep nights out on the town. If money is an issue, ask family or friends to babysit or look for parents'-night-out ministries.

We've done one of those all-inclusive trips to Mexico, with the towels on the bed made into swans and a nice hot tub. I'm all about hot tubs. Our first night there, I used way too much soap, and the bubbles were flying, but it got us laughing, loosened up, and in the mood to reconnect. We slept well, ate well, and read books that are more than twenty pages. Another time, we went to a cabin, built fires, hiked, hot-tubbed, and sat under the stars in the biting cold with a glass of wine. And no one was there to interrupt our conversation. The quiet nearly killed us, and we talked too much about our kids.

The Parable of Thrown Confetti

Marriage reminds me of the parable of the sower, the way we can choose to be fertile soil for God to guide our spiritual transformation.

I updated the parable a teeny bit and inserted self, this fiery me-girl who car dances (and I don't care if you see me at the stoplight). I renamed it "the parable of the confetti thrower."

Jesus, that way-too-generous Messiah, spreads love like confetti being thrown at a party. Confetti, like seed, can land anywhere. When it's thrown in a crowd, some of it lands on the floor to be swept up and thrown away. Then some of it sticks to shoes and travels to who knows where. Some simply falls into places where it will never see the light of day. Thank heavens, though, some of that sparkly stuff sticks to those who are really taking some risks out there at the party: dancing, moving through the world with joy, embracing others, even when it's so obvious we're all imperfect and clumsy, just trying to practice our moves and to get in step with one another.

Marriage is an opportunity to practice some indulgent, gracious love, like God does, scattering it like a wild man—or woman. It's Jesus at the party throwing confetti. I imagine that the sparkly slivers of divine love settle in our hair and on our skin but mostly in our eyes, changing our perceptions, so that we open wide our arms to the spouse who is a far cry from us. Marriage is an opportunity to love with abandon and get bathed in bits of Jesus's confetti.

CHAPTER 8

THE ANNUAL SIBLING CHRISTMAS COCOON COOKIE BAKE-OFF

After taking the bread and giving thanks, [Jesus] broke it and gave it to them, saying, "This is my body, which is given for you. Do this in remembrance of me."
—Luke 22:19

When I was a kid, our family used to watch "Bonanza." I really liked having a Sunday night TV ritual.
—Anne Lamott

Normally, it's balmy in my home state during the month of December, but there are exceptions. A few years ago, freezing weather actually landed in the middle of our smallish southern city. Many side roads were closed, and the church parking lot was a solid sheet of ice. I should have bought that snow shovel, the one that made me laugh hysterically while shopping at a neighbor's garage sale.

The exceptional weather meant no one could get to the church building safely, so a techie helped me arrange for plan B. We would stream a devotional online from my home with my family as we lit the second Advent candle. We wouldn't be in the beautiful sanctuary, but we could all be safe and warm and connected.

On my end, it meant I had to get the laptop set up near our Christmas tree, with a view of our own Advent wreath in the shot, showing the four traditional candles to mark the season and the center candle that represented Christ. My cell phone served as a monitor, so that I could view what the online worshipers were seeing and hearing. My husband gathered our boys, who sat nearby, curious at our makeshift altar.

As we went live online, I welcomed those who had joined us. Getting prepared for Jesus to come, I began to talk about the season of Advent. I then read some words appropriate for the second Sunday, probably one of the Gospels' sermons about repentance and cleansing fire from John the Baptist.

While trying to juggle the whole candle-lighting production, I noticed that one of the boys was watching our faces on my computer screen. Wyatt leaned into the camera shot between the computer screen and the Advent candles, which had already been lit. Trying very hard not to move the makeshift equipment, I tried to catch Victor's eye to communicate the worrisome situation unfolding in real time with a particular starstruck child. As my sweet spouse prepared to corral him, Wyatt said, "Something smells funny."

Something did smell funny.

It's singed hair, I thought. *Oh no, my child's hair is on fire!* My child's hair was on fire.

> *Sisters, we are born into rituals, and we make them, from small sacred moments to grand celebrations.*

Fire (and stuff on fire) has a way of catching our attention. Maybe John the Baptist's sermons and crazy rituals really do help us pay attention to what matters most.

To this day, those alarming, comic moments of trying to celebrate Advent remind me of the ending of the classic holiday movie *A Christmas Story*. Ralphie's father had been waiting all Christmas day for the roast turkey, only to have the neighbor's dogs steal it off the kitchen table. The family ends up having their holiday dinner at the local Chinese restaurant. Although Peking duck is not on the typical American Christmas menu, Ralphie's weirdly normal family is thoughtfully serenaded with some verses of "Deck the Halls." The Chinese American waitstaff tries to make this crazy Christmas derailment meaningful with a chorus of "fa la la la la, la la la la!"

I have a pastor friend who takes his family to eat Chinese food every Christmas Day because he's insanely funny and because pastors and their families are exhausted on Christmas Day, even more so than Santa. We birth Jesus and bring the presents in the same night.

Similarly, I pause and embrace the moment every December when I see a neighbor's picture window displaying a fish-net-stockinged leg lamp, a nod to the same movie. I love that leg because it's on the crass, tacky, and especially, fleshy side of life. And life, particularly family life, isn't sanitized. At any moment, the ride can turn brutally painful or brightly beautiful.

I view the tantalizing, bold leg as a solid way to de-sterilize Christmas and family from what's trending on the tree and to sit with our human messes, confusion, and imperfection. It's my belief that Jesus didn't come for the cleaned-up sparkles. He sits cross-legged in the floor, tinsel in his tangled hair, cookie crumbs hanging off his beard, and bits of Play-Doh stuck to his modest shirt. He sits with us in the middle of loud, spoiled children, having overheard that thing you shouldn't say to a spouse during the season of God becoming one of us. Or loving me in the midst of my coziness with what I know to be an unnecessary materialistic freak show. It's just that I love me some holiday swag and matching bedazzled family sweaters.

Sisters, we are born into rituals, and we make them, from small sacred moments to grand celebrations. In her book *Grounded*, Diana Butler Bass reminds us that the words *habit* and *habitat* are from the same Latin root, meaning "to hold or possess." As the nearest of neighbors, the immediate family with whom we live and dwell gives us opportunity to regularly practice important behavior we will take into the world: "sharing, eating together, praying, conversation, critical thinking, acceptance and forgiveness, and charity." In other words, how we perform domestic rituals, how we lean into and sustain traditions, and how we foster habits at home that shape who we are and affect the wide world beyond (God's world).

The necessity for such grounding is especially welcome when families are up to their elbows in chaos, from daily routines to seasonal slogs, like the gargantuan task (and very unspiritual pilgrimage) of back-to-school shopping. No matter what the source of family busyness or chores, we all need the steady rhythm of singing our thanks around the meal, which, in our kitchen may accompany a cacophony of pots banging, laughter, screams, and, yep, thrown food. (Maybe that's why we continue to call low-lying food grub.)

Locate and Hallow the Sacred Family Portals

My boys have always been fascinated by keys and locks with combinations. When I was a little girl, I had a secret diary that locked, a jewelry box with a key, and a treasure chest I once ordered from a cereal box. I don't think it's unusual for kids to keep objects with a certain reverence. I believe it is the beginning of connecting particular, treasured memories to the minutia of life. Sifting through our keepsakes reminds us of important information and mirrors the way we'll decide to hold onto a valuable time during our spirit journey and continue to reflect on what we keep and let its meaning shape us.

After moving my mom to a care facility, my siblings and I cleaned out her home. I took some of her books, which can tell you a great deal about a person. My mom liked fiction, theology, biography, politics, and current events. I received Mom's punch bowl, which had many times held a lime-green-colored frothy drink made of sherbet and ginger ale. I took her VCR-taped movie collection, to help me recall her taste in movies and her neat, cursive writing across the labels. I ended up with some boxes of cherished family photos, dating back to my great-grandparents. Victor and I adopted her blind thirteen-year-old cocker spaniel, Daisy, an aging, red-furred creature who was snippy, was spoiled to food scraps, smelled perpetually, and lived, to our astonishment, another three years.

More important to me, Sister Gayle also put aside the red, round, wooden Christmas tray for my family. I cannot remember a Christmas without the presence of that tray. In old English letters, it announces, *Christmas in the country, Christmas in the town, Christmas in our hearts, Christmas all around.* Schmaltzy *and* sacrosanct is a thing.

When Sister placed the red tray in my hands, she blessed me with something she knew connected me to the past, to Mom, and to my history. It was something I would use with my children. It offered one way to keep our family story going and, with it, who we are becoming. It's never merely about physical objects; memories accompany the physical objects and support the rituals and traditions we need in a culture in which everything is changing at a speed faster than most of us can accommodate or embrace.

An uncle of the boys made a wooden box in a distinct color for each one and painted each boy's name on his box. These boxes store shells from the beach, fossils from family hikes, found seeds, shiny metal from a park, a birthday card here and there, some stickers, loose beads, a tube or two of glitter glue, bottle caps, and even parts of past Halloween costumes. This childhood collection is the beginning of what matters to my boys as they gather the ingredients of their stories. At some point, one of them may take hold of the red Christmas tray and make it a symbol of hospitality, welcome, or Christmas, a symbol first held by their grandmother, then their mother. Or maybe they'll hallow the platter they made for me, a design with four red elf socks that the boys made from their own footprints.

OK, my red tray will probably go to Goodwill. Although it would be nice if I got a daughter-in-law who is either an anthropologist or archaeologist. I'm really open to a good therapist too.

Family Movie Night as Spiritual Practice

Every family is different, which makes how we live and work and play unique. The ways me and mine strengthen our bond aren't yours. Some families have game nights or sport nights, but with our tribe, one of our big bonding moments are movie nights.

As our boys have grown, we have set aside Friday evenings as our end-of-the-week celebration. Sometimes, we'll go see a new release at the theater on a Friday afternoon and enjoy the big bucket of popcorn, the candy, and a cool, dark theatre with a huge screen and reclining chairs. But most often, we settle in together on the red couch in the den with throws. Some nights, I make cookies for us, or sometimes we gather around bowls of cheese dip, dripping across the glass coffee table and chins.

Porches, doors, tables, and words of welcome are sacred materials with which to build families and relations.

I believe watching movies and talking about the characters may offer us ways to overcome obstacles, to deal with people who are different from us, and to examine our fears (fears of loneliness, rejection, loss, and death). I believe this about books as well. There was the night we watched *The Little Princess*. As it became clear that the amnesiac father in the story might not recognize his little girl, who was screaming for him after their long separation, I looked to see every child of mine with tears streaming down his cheeks. These powerful reactions make it possible for us to talk about the hard things we might not otherwise explore as a family.

There is also a past lodged in our particular ritual. I sat next to my mother on the couch many Saturday evenings while we watched old classics. She taught me to appreciate Humphrey Bogart, Katharine Hepburn, Gregory Peck, Jimmy Stewart, Olivia de Havilland, and Cary Grant. "Oh, Honey," she'd say, "I first saw this picture down at…" It was some theater that no longer existed and where, she claimed, you could watch a double feature for a dime. Even when I was home from college, we watched the networks' airing of *The Sound of Music* or *The Wizard of Oz*. Each time, we worried about the von Trapp family's escape or Dorothy getting home to Kansas, not to mention the secret desires of growing up, being accepted, and learning what bravery might look like.

Mom wasn't a snob, though. She liked new stuff too. She was so into the first *Star Wars* movie, she gave me a light saber that Christmas, for which I was too old. OK, it was a really long plastic flashlight, but I knew it meant more. The gift was implicitly about her strong belief in the triumph of good over evil and the implicit nod to the light in the darkness.

The last movie we took Mom to see was *Toy Story 3*. A grown-up Andy is headed off to college. What will become of his favorite toys, friends who have been with him all his life? Will Andy throw them away, or will he pass them along to another child? I cannot watch this movie without crying. At the end, my boys look back at me, knowing that joy and sorrow are sometimes mixed together. It's all mashed up in my trembling lower lip and the tears that fall: Mom, movies, love, loss, and the next chapter of life.

We're not finished figuring out our sacred practices as the boys grow and we get older, not by any means. As our family identity and story unfold, we search not only for the pacifier, the lovies, or the smell of rosemary that roots us and comforts us, but also for the game changers and the steady practices that will make us stronger and better humans.

Come in This House

When my mother opened the door to greet any of her family or close friends, and whoever happened to be hanging around the door, she'd say, "Hello, Darlin'! Come on in this house!" It meant not only that she was glad to see whoever was at the door but also that they belonged. She had their back and a glass of sweet tea with lemon.

Sister says a version of this welcome when we bring our boys to her house. "Look who's here! It's *my* boys!"

Words carry the power to provide security, safety, and hospitality. Jesus was exceptional at this sort of neighborly practice, making himself available to those who might be disconnected outliers.

Jesus announced he had sinners covered, even tax collectors like Zacchaeus, saying, "Man, come on down from that tree. We're going to talk eye-to-eye. I'm eating at your house today!" And when some folks at Simon the Leper's table were having dinner, they scolded a woman and called her wasteful when she anointed Jesus with precious oil. Jesus retorted, "Leave her alone." He declared her ritual a moment of spiritual awareness, ministering to him before his death, and an act that would always be remembered.

Porches, doors, tables, and words of welcome are sacred materials with which to build families and relations.

Some years ago, we finally had enough money to redo the pool in our backyard. Believe me, the cement pond wasn't impressive. The coping was falling in, the paint was peeling, and the tile was falling off. It seemed romantic when we bought it; starlit couple nights, a glass of wine, and all that. But we had other household issues to consider when children and expenses started piling up.

When we finally got it rehabbed, my husband declared that we would begin having weekend afternoon swims with whoever might want to join us. He invited friends who were single parents, people we didn't know from our neighborhood, families from school or the ice rink, a little boy who rides his bike to our house without his parents on occasion, and, frankly, whomever he wanted to invite. The pool rally became his ritual, a gift to our kids and others, and a place to gather with no strings and lots of love.

One Saturday, I had chores to do and wasn't around until late in the afternoon. When I got home, I found eleven children in our pool. Some were diving off their dads' shoulders, others were jumping from the sides, and some were nibbling snacks someone had laid out, all under the watchful eye of an assortment of people—Christian, Hindu, agnostic, white, black, brown, single, and married. I was somewhat horrified at the sheer number of people, wondering if we needed a permit of some kind for this size of a gathering. At the same time, I was quietly overjoyed by my husband's desire to welcome people and create neighborly rituals for our boys to participate in and remember.

To be honest, I need rest from people because I'm a pastor and I do people nonstop. I'm not all-in every time my spouse wants to send out the call for a pool party, but that's OK. I know these get-togethers are crazily sacred and chaos to be cherished. Our guests may not find me offering freshly baked brownies at the door when they arrive, but everyone is welcome.

In the very last chapter of the Gospel of John, Peter and some of the disciples decide to go back on the Sea of Galilee for a little fishing, just like the old days, as was their habit and vocation. When reading that passage, I've always thought that the followers were struggling with what to do next, not sure how to move ahead without the physical presence of Jesus. Yet when they gather and fish and eat together, it comes back to them—the memory and the purpose to feed a bigger world.

Ways and Words to Soothe the Savage Beast

Mom used to drive me crazy with a proverbial phrase that completely reversed a negative dynamic. OK, my negative dynamic.

I hadn't thought of it for decades until, one day, my oldest was in a giant pout. Penn's bottom lip was out so far he could have carried more stuff than my biggest bucket-style bag. I wanted to scold him and lecture him. I wanted to tell him how good his life is because I know that always works great with kids who have very little ability to compare their experience to that of others. At least when they are, say, five years old. It'd be great if we could transplant the hard life learnings that way, but we can't. And when I'm a big, fat hot mess and impatient from too much work, giving to others, and without enough self-care, it's hard to put my foot down in workable ways and not in my mouth. I had to reframe the moment. Add a bit of light and salt.

Suddenly, Penn's horrible, even affected mood struck me as funny, as did his contorted little face. So, as sweetly and annoyingly as possible, with sugar, honey, and fructose on top, I looked him in his angry, sad eyes and said those wonderful words that my mom used to say: "Smiling comes so easy. Do not wear a frown. If you feel one rising, always smile it down."

Naturally, the key ingredient in reciting this bit for maximum effect is to say it in the most sickening Glinda-the-Good-Witch type of voice as possible.

And what happened when I said the magic words? Low and behold, it was like an angel of the Lord appeared and placed a coal to his sullen lips because that grumpy boy broke a smile without any harsh words. Courtesy and points scored, Grandma.

The people who spend a lot of time being emotionally healthy, God love them; know that my mom's gift was a simple proverb to diffuse the situation. As our kids grow, we can model our favorite methods for handling stress and chaos. Everyone has a sweet spot. Some of us learn we can sit with a purring cat or splash cold water in our face or exercise aggressively for five minutes to take the edge off, but humor passed down is like a bottle of champagne uncorked, full of concentrated positrons unleashed for just the right moment.

When I'm with my siblings, we have a litany we recite of Mom-isms that bond us from the Matriarch down:

"I'll give you something to cry about."

"I'm no short-order cook!"

"Do you think I was born yesterday?"

"Just scrape off the burnt part."

"Who do you think you are?"

"If you don't have anything nice to say, don't say anything at all!"

"Put some calamine lotion on it."

The Recipe

Even though Mom died, many of her words and habits live on through us, but how do we sustain that sassy spirit and continue to celebrate the family that remains? One of my brothers decided we should institute the Annual Sibling Christmas Cocoon Cookie Bake-Off.

Mom had perfected a cookie recipe, and for years she baked and gave out those cookies the weeks before Christmas. Each of us was given a tin of homemade shortbread cookies, which had been rolled between her fingers in the shape of a cocoon or crescent and doused in powdered sugar. There is not another Christmas cookie that compares, not in our family.

That's why, very early in January each year, all of my siblings and I make an enormously big deal out of our competition to see who can deliver the best cocoon, one worthy of the name. Our event is always held after Christmas when we're less harried, so that we can all bring a soup or dip and a big platter of our own version of Mom's classic cookie. There are real-live judges, a blind tasting, the countdown, the reveal, and the honorary platter, given to that year's grand champion, followed by a stream of Facebook posts and boasts. The siblings' meal together is for the big people, but my children help me with baking the cookies, and they get the message. Remembering, eating, loving, forgiving, and laughing are to be done consistently: daily, weekly, in small ways, in big ways, and with others.

No matter what's happening in life, Jesus has some guidelines for building community and family. I think we ought to try them regularly, though not necessarily in any specific order.

Take, eat. Be nourished together with me, says Jesus.

When rejected (or defeated), shake the dust from your feet, literally, and move forward.

Similarly, pick up your mat. (The family may need exercise.)

Light a lamp for self or others, or maybe a nice candle.

Be salt; spice it up.

Wash when dirty.

Anoint with oil.

Head to the hills.

Don't pile up what you don't need. (It's so exhausting to take care of.)

Listen to stories.

Remember what's important.

Note

Diana Butler Bass, *Grounded* (New York: HarperOne, 2015), 179–81.

The Famous Singleton Christmas Cocoon Cookies
(as written out by my Mom)

2 sticks of softened butter
⅓ cup powdered sugar
2 tsp. water
1 tsp. vanilla
2 cups flour
¼ tsp. salt (optional)
1 cup chopped pecans

Cream butter and sugar; add water and vanilla. Mix well. Blend in flour, salt, and nuts. Chill four hours and shape into crescent shapes. Bake on ungreased cookie sheets at 275 degrees for about an hour. Remove from pan and roll in powdered sugar!

CHAPTER 9

THE WISDOM OF ALBUS DUMBLEDORE

*The light shines in the darkness, and the darkness
doesn't extinguish the light.*
—John 1:5

*Happiness can be found, even in the darkest of times,
if one remembers to turn on the light.*
—*Albus Dumbledore,* Harry Potter and the Prisoner of Azkaban

I love to drive a stick shift. Go ahead. Call me old-fashioned, but I can drive cars anywhere in Europe, surely a necessary skill. Booyakasha!

Actually, a long time ago, I chose a Zen car experience: to be one with the transmission. That's why it nearly killed my NASCAR spirit when we traded in my ancient Saab convertible for a van to haul kids. Suddenly, I felt like that teacher in *The Magic School Bus* books. Similar to Ms. Frizzle, whose name I physically resemble, I was hopping around our family time zones (known as The Schedule) on a bus full of sticky, sassy, cramped kids.

Vans don't promote Zen car experiences because they are filled mostly—at least mine is—with screaming boys "touching" (that is, elbowing and punching) one another and accusing one another of multiple offenses every two seconds; not to mention the stuff I've found under the seats and in cup holders. Think fermentation. A friend got me a referee shirt and yellow flag to throw, but it's hard to foul people when you're driving. The alarming reality is that you never truly know what's happening behind your driver's seat. See no evil.

Once, I took my church staff on a continuing education trip in my van. The children's minister was in the back. He pointed out that someone in our family had written on the back of the leather seats. I had no idea. Yet another incident beyond my control. "Oh yeah," he said, very nonchalantly. "That's chieroglyphics" (a mashup of *children* and *hieroglyphics*) explaining the enigmatic symbols scrawled by sneaky young children on your most expensive items. If Google ever gets those autonomous cars out there, there will be a power shift.

Finally, Sisters, I got another standard-transmission car that made room for all the boys who no longer needed car seats, just boosters. They love to ride in Momma's car. Not long ago, we pulled into the driveway after a trip to the store, just me and two boys singing and car dancing all the way home. I was headed into our house and enjoying myself tremendously when Wyatt yelled that the car was moving without a driver. I turned to look and was stunned to see my nonthreatening little car going backward down our driveway toward the street. I dropped my ice coffee, my purse, and my sacks and phone, and I chased the car until it was almost in the street, where I grabbed the door, hopped in, and applied the brakes. Penn was still in the car. Somewhere in my head, in a matter of seconds, I thought that, maybe, I'd only lose my foot and save Penn.

*It's **how** we talk about and model handling the dangers and disasters that will ultimately equip our children.*

That's the thing, isn't it? How do you keep these buggers safe? After Penn was born, one of the first overwhelming inclinations I had was to protect him at all costs. *Suck it up, Buttercup. You're in charge.* And even when I thought I was being very careful, the most bizarre, scary, and unpleasant things happened because life doesn't go as planned.

Take, for instance, the time I had Penn in a baby marshmallow chair, a fairly new product that we'd gotten from someone at a baby shower. It looked helpful to me and was said to help with a baby's sitting-up muscles. I squeezed the baby inside the snugly, squishy, short seat, watching as his fat baby legs protruded. He looked very perky and happy. He was supposed to stay put.

While carefully watching him lounge on the large kitchen island, I turned for the proverbial one second to retrieve something from the sink when I heard a loud thump. He'd arched his back, popped out of the puffy chair, and fallen facedown next to the chair, but still on the island. If Baby Penn had gone forward, he'd have fallen on our brick floors. Brick is hard.

I grabbed up my crying child, "Oh Baby, Oh Baby! Momma is so sorry, so sorry." After a few minutes, he smiled and laughed, like the whole thing was some silly test of my nerves. I'd gotten a reprieve, but I was mad at myself and the scary chair. Bad chair!

That was not the last time there was an equipment malfunction. Another time we had to cut our baby out of a bathtub seat contraption when his legs were stuck into the wrong holes. My husband used pruning shears—yes, pruning shears—to literally cut out our screaming baby from his tub and to calm his hyperventilating mom.

At four, Wyatt cut open his head while removing his shirt. Yes, we had a clothing accident. He leaned forward and banged his head on the table, perfectly slicing open his hairline and requiring stitches.

At two-and-a-half, Sullivan secretly sucked on a cap from a bottle of milk while I was strolling him (and three others) through the National Air and Space Museum. We were having a good time until a stranger told me the baby was choking, which I couldn't see.

Each time there's some drama, I consider what might have happened, what could happen, and what has happened to other families in a split second. My stomach goes knotty and my heart beats like I just fell from one of those parachute rides.

In my ministry, I have known parents who have suffered through the loss of a child, sometimes because of a sudden illness, an unde-tected aneurysm, an incident of choking, or a fall from a tree.

Bad Stuff Stinks, but It Demands Notice

When I was a young associate pastor, I often gave the message for the brief children's time during morning worship. Most adults, espe-cially parents, either cringe during this time or find it delightfully entertaining.

It's not usually described as the "serious" part of worship. Once, my friend Susan, a talented teacher, loaned me her crazy Halloween hat to wear as I described All Hallows' Eve and its connection to All Saints' Day. Another time, I hid a "lost" sheep in the chancel area and encour-aged the children to do everything they could do to find that one poor sheep gone astray.

One Sunday, I decided to talk to the children about something scary that was all over the news. I didn't want to frighten them, but I believe there are times when we need to model how to deal with dif-ficult realities so that our children are equipped to cope emotionally with bad news and to respond as Christians. After all, in my tradition, our baptismal vows ask us to be ready to confront the powers and prin-cipalities—the bad stuff around us: *Do you renounce the spiritual forces of wickedness, reject the evil powers of this world, and repent of your sin?* Such promises leave us little room for retreating below a blanket of comfort and denial.

Here was my difficult topic: I spoke about the American Embassy bombing in Nairobi, Kenya, but I promise I spoke carefully. I talked about a hard thing not only because the horror was all over the news but also because our own United Methodist bishop was in Kenya at the time. What we know now is that particular act of violence signaled the beginning of a new, volatile conflict around the world. (Dealing with terrorism and its proponents would not go away quietly or be tucked in a safe pocket.)

In those few moments with our church's children, I wanted to reassure the children regarding the images they might be seeing on television. I also wanted to explain that good things were also happening in Kenya for hurting people because The United Methodist Church was at work on their behalf in that country.

The next week I got a call from some parents, very fine people, who were disturbed that I had mentioned the bombing during the children's time. They explained that church is a time of escape, safety, and security for their children, not a time for harsh and brutal reality.

At the time of our conversation, I had no children, so I wondered if I would feel as they did. If I had my own beautiful children, would I think, as I did then, that it was much more important to acknowledge inexplicable horrific events and proclaim that God was with us even during the bad times? Or would I also naturally desire to shield my children from the harshness and violence of the world?

The year before the Nairobi bombing, J. K. Rowling's first novel, *Harry Potter and the Sorcerer's Stone*, was released. I purchased the book for my youngest nephew. After the third book was released, I bought the available books for myself and read them during my vacation. Eventually, as each was released, I read them all and have continued to read them with my boys. Let's just say that my children rock when it comes to playing *Harry Potter Trivial Pursuit*. Here, I pause to brag. After we opened the game and began calling out Potter-themed trivia questions, Aubrey correctly identified the name of the obscure love potion mentioned in Professor Slughorn's Potions class: Amortentia.

He beamed. I felt as if he had won the Pulitzer Prize for Literary Awareness by a seven-year-old.

My favorite Potter character is Professor Albus Dumbledore, the headmaster of Hogwarts School of Witchcraft and Wizardry. *Albus*, from the Latin, means "bright or white." As a pastor, that got my attention because I often wear a liturgical robe called an alb, which, in the tradition of the early church, symbolizes baptism and resurrection. Dumbledore is a character who often fights the darkness that threatens to engulf the wizarding world, or any world.

In discussing Dumbledore as the central mentor found in the books, Rowling has been quoted as saying, "Dumbledore is a very wise man who knows that Harry is going to have to learn a few hard lessons to prepare him for what may be coming in his life. He allows Harry to get into what he wouldn't allow another pupil to do, and he also unwillingly permits Harry to confront things he'd rather protect him from."

Professor Dumbledore's greatest wisdom is in acknowledging that evil is real and that part of the human journey is to renounce it and, possibly, to fight it. One of the values I like most about the books is their willingness to name evil and refuse evil as the last and final word.

What surprised me most about some of the initial criticism of the popular books was the objection by certain Christians that the Harry Potter books are about magic and the occult when the books are instead clearly about something more frightening: the struggle between goodness and evil, life and death, hate and love. Whether we want our children to know about bad stuff is not the issue. It's *how* we talk about and model handling the dangers and disasters that will ultimately equip our children.

Use Your Super, Simple Mom Powers

Shopping can be dangerous. It was the end of summer. A local department store was having a great sale. Thank heavens we have almost all guys in our house so that fashion changes are minimal, not that my man doesn't care about fashion. Everyone in our state knows he wears themed neckties, including soccer, flag, faces of cute children, and even Cat in the Hat; in other words, normal statement ties for a sixty-nine-year-old doctor, lawyer, and political type of guy. Once I begged him to change his school-themed tie before attending a Rosanne Cash concert at the governor's mansion. Johnny Cash's talented daughter was in town to raise money for her father's boyhood home in Dyess, Arkansas. I was dressed in all black, which seemed the superior way to honor the daughter of the "man in black." When we stepped up to get our picture with the singer and songwriter, she betrayed me. "Oh, look at that cool tie!" she said and seemed to mean it. *I trusted you, Roseanne!*

So, on this shopping trip, it was with great fortitude that I took my three-year-old to buy Daddy some clothes. I tried to move quickly, gathering up undies, T-shirts, dress shirts, a couple of ties, and blue jeans. I knew all my friends and neighbors would certainly be glad to see Victor in a decent pair of jeans. He tends to wear them until they're hanging by a denim thread. And when I suggest he dispose of them, he says they are a sign of his ability to make fashion (he may be the oldest hipster I know). "Most people pay big money for this look," he tells me. Gigantic sigh.

> *I can't ignore crucial Bible stories that refer to the presence of evil in the world.*

Penn's behavior at the store was good, but he was at that three-ish stage during which he loved running through the clothing racks. I remember doing that when I was kid, running through the bolts of fabric and seeing if my older sister, who was also trying to corral her children, could find me. Believe me, she's yucking it up now.

As Penn darted in and out of clothing, he begged to go up the escalator. We'd just been to DC a few weeks earlier and maneuvered escalators at the airport and the metro. We'd taught him when to step on the escalator and when and how to exit. We had cautioned him about keeping his feet on the middle of the escalator. He'd done quite well. So I promised we'd go up and down the escalator before we left the store.

The sales clerk in the department offered to hold our giant bag while we rode the escalator, the final treat before heading home and the payoff for waiting on Mommy. As we stepped on the escalator, I reminded Penn not to take his eyes off the steps, but midway through, he did. He had his back to the step as we ascended. I called to him two or three times to turn around, and he finally did and stepped off nicely, but it took a little too long for him to respond—a toddler, developmental wiring issue.

After stepping off, we turned around to make our descent. Everything was going well. I'd gotten my husband's clothes and entertained our three-year-old with no major incident. I'd get home in a little over an hour. The time factor always weighed on me when there were three babies at home and help was so limited.

Just as I saw Penn's right foot on the side of the escalator and was just about to tell him to take his foot off the side of the moving stair, he started a panicked whimper. I pulled his foot, and it didn't readily yield his camouflage Mickey Mouse Croc. His foot was stuck. All of my mom wisdom about everything from BB guns to electrical outlets came back to me. Giant letters in bold red: escalators really *are* dangerous.

I grabbed and pulled harder. Penn grew more panicked. Finally, the Croc came loose and so did my child's foot. We were descending fast. As we stepped off, Penn let out a death scream, followed by a silence that was long enough to take a breath before he screamed some more. I pulled off the mauled Croc, which had a big gash across the top, but there was no blood. Best I could tell, the Croc was bit, but the child was OK—on the outside. It was fear that still had hold of him.

"Are you crying because you're scared?" I asked. He nodded furiously. I held him at the bottom of the escalator right in front of the makeup counters where distracted clerks gave him empathetic glances.

After the crying subsided, I said, "We're going up again." Of course, this suggestion was met with panic, but I explained we would start with Mommy carrying him.

"Penn, we have to get back on this horse, or you'll be scared of the escalator next time we need to use one."

I picked him up and put him down as we went up. He allowed this independence, stating, "We have da keep our feets in da middle of dese stairs."

That's right, Honey.

The Dumbledore Approach

Since the terrorist violence in Kenya years ago, there have been many more instances of terror, war, and natural disaster, some in our own country, some around the world. There have been close calls and actual events.

As a momma, not as a pastor, I have had the opportunity to decide if I would talk with my children about difficult and deadly things, or not. Of course, certain disclosure depends on a child's developmental stage.

Because I'm the sort of Christian who thinks everyone would benefit from a reality check with a good therapist to talk about the hard stuff, I can't ignore crucial Bible stories that refer to the presence of evil in the world: Herod's slaughter of the innocents, Stephen's murder, or Jesus's execution. As Martin Luther King Jr. once told the Ebenezer Baptist congregation he served, the church collectively must acknowledge Good Friday, or it cannot truly heal people. It reminds me of the way I loved playing ball in our yard in summer. The yard was very green but contained awful stickers, barely noticeable until you are splayed across them in a slide. Woe to those who slide across those sticky patches.

About the time of the shopping trip with Penn, Haiti was devastated by an earthquake. It was almost impossible to protect a child completely from the images of the people in Haiti. I received word that one of my own Methodist colleagues had died in a hotel that collapsed. He was there working on poverty issues.

I was not working in a local church at the time. I was on disability from heart failure. But the following Sunday after the earthquake, we visited a worship service with our big baby crew in tow.

As we settled in, the children's minister mentioned Haiti's plight in her time with the young ones. She also demonstrated how to make health kits to send to Haiti to be distributed to those in need. As a momma, I found myself relieved that this woman mentioned the Haitians and the earthquake in church and gave the children a sense that they could help people in need. Déjà vu.

I confess I didn't turn off the TV news or shield my three-year-old from all the images, though I was careful to control the amount of viewing time and content. I watched some of the news of Haiti with him, and we talked about it. I tried to provide a context. The minister's words from Sunday actually reinforced the conversation we'd had about ways to help those in difficult circumstances, emphasizing that is our calling as Christians.

The next week, on the way home from his dance class, Penn suddenly started talking about "the ersquake people." Maybe it was because I often have public radio on in the car when I first pick him up at school. Perhaps the reporter said something about Haiti that I didn't hear. But my boy began suggesting that we not only make the health kit but also send food and water. "Don't forget the water," he said very seriously, "that's very, very, very important."

I very much want to shield my children from the hard stuff of life, but I also want to equip them to face pain. It is a fine line that we parents walk, tiptoeing across the high wire of safety and risk, contributing to the healthful formation of a human being.

Penn also heard me tell his daddy that we ought to consider getting a Haitian child because "what would one more in our home be?" To which Penn replied, "I sink we cud prabubly do *two* more babies."

Always Carry Band-Aids

We didn't get any more babies, not of the human kind. Instead, we continued to load up on dogs. I've always had dogs, but a surprising reality is that your children are not you. At some point, we had to accept that Penn was a cat person. Although we weren't particularly keen on more animals, Victor and I decided that a seven-year-old could have his own pet and, with it, the incumbent litter box, feeding, and play required to house and care for a domestic animal.

I searched listings on a local rescue group's website. We went to the vet who had a litter of tuxedo kittens listed. Penn was enamored with one very small kitten. She was predominantly white, with black swaths and a striking mark down her nose, as if she'd sniffed a permanent black marker and missed.

Penn decided to adopt her, so we scheduled further shots and worming. The doctor gave us a box, like a Build-A-Bear carryall, and we headed to a local pet store for food, a collar, treats, and toys. On the way home, I asked my child, "What are you going to name her?" He thought of some names like Snow and Ice. I suggested she looked like a Sonic Blizzard, made of vanilla ice cream with chunks of Oreo thrown around. He liked that.

Blizzard was a sweet kitten. Penn held her almost all the time. He snuggled with her, sat with her, read to her, and cared for her. By Christmas, it became apparent that Blizzard was not getting bigger, and she was not playing like a crazy, feet-flying, spasmodic creature on catnip.

The vet offered several diseases, none of which were very good. It soon became clear that Blizzard had the one stupid kitty illness that wasn't going to get better. That began the conversation about when to put her to sleep, and that conversation included our boy.

Our vet was proud of us, he said, because his parents made his animals disappear when they were old. He grew up thinking his pets didn't like him. Rather than helping him process loss, his parents had led him to believe that his pets were just happier elsewhere. When he told me this horror story, I concluded, *No wonder you're a vet! Unresolved!* Still, I understood why his parents wanted to protect him from losing a beloved member of the family.

Penn decided he wanted to be with his kitten when she was put down. I explained that he could be with her the whole time. I told him her doctor would give Blizzard a little shot that would not hurt and would put her to sleep forever. I explained that being with Blizzard at the end might be hard, but he could be with her the whole time, and we would be with him. I didn't explain that this loss was going to hurt him, like a pebble rubbing against his tender little heart, until that pebble is slowly worn smooth, and his sadness ebbs and is replaced more often by memories of love.

My sweet child remained to the end, with heartbreaking cries. I've cried for my own pets, each so unique and intertwined with a particular time in my life, but it was different to see my son experience his own Good Friday. I looked up at Victor, and we were both crying. Our own gift was simply to be there. We could not make it better.

Some weeks later, we visited the animal shelter. I'd been there the day the city had opened it and dedicated it. The prayer I gave at that event was about caring for all animals and still hangs on the wall of the facility.

We were escorted to the cat section. There was one kitten, a tabby, nothing like Blizzard, but he stole Penn's heart. On the way home Penn immediately named him Cougar.

Cougar didn't snuggle as much as the sick little kitten had. He was too healthy. He played and danced across and under furniture. It soon became clear to Penn that he had not replaced Blizzard. He continued to cry for her, especially in the evenings before bed. I rubbed his back and told him how sorry I was. We ordered a stone marker for the place on the hillside of our yard where we buried Blizzard. A friend from church painted him a picture of his first kitten to be hung in his room. At some point, I purchased Penn a few books from Erin Hunter's cat series, *The Warrior Clan*. I learned that in the cat world, I'm a two-legged.

Cougar has grown into a big tabby guy who sits on my computer and my lap. He talks to me. I've seen how he's taken a different place in my son's heart. Penn is older and wiser and has trained his friend to come for treats and pets. When I recently went through a bad patch at work, Cougar sat for hours on my bed. The only downside of having Cougar is that all those allergy shots I had years ago as a kid have worn off. I am allergic to this cat and have asthma for the first time in my life. People have told me we should get rid of the cat, but he's family. So I go get the shots, use my inhaler, and practice finding light in the darkness by means of an ordinary tabby cat who loves us. That cat is sometimes the sacred Band-Aid to my own wounds, and my rescued self.

Blessed Are the Tears

One of the most moving scenes in the Harry Potter series is when Harry learns that Professor Severus Snape is not in alignment with the evil wizard Lord Voldemort and instead actually made the greatest sacrifice of all. As Snape dies, he tells Harry to collect his tears, that Harry might use them to magically understand his story. Snape not only truly loved Harry's mother, Lily Potter, but also vowed to do whatever Dumbledore asked of him to protect Harry, even while appearing to be an accomplice of evil. Instead, Snape gives his own life for others. Years later, Harry names his son Albus Severus Potter.

Life is often much more complex and layered than we're willing to acknowledge, not only to ourselves but also to our children. Wouldn't it be better for mothers not to wipe the tears completely, but to collect them and hold them, to process the hidden nooks and crannies we cram to the back, where the light is not so bright and we are not known so fully?

I love a particular line in Psalm 56, which is a lament.

> You yourself have kept track of my misery.
> Put my tears into your bottle—
> aren't they on your scroll already? (v. 8)

No matter what, God suffers with us, the true meaning of the word *compassion*. That's how God loves us, by respecting our tears, by collecting them not as a waste, but as part of our story. Tears are certainly part of our biblical story, the way Jesus weeps over his dear friend Lazarus, and the way he cries over the sacred city of Jerusalem that fails to heed God's message. Life and death bring tears, but they also bring happiness.

Note

J. K. Rowling at the Royal Albert Hall, interview by Stephen Fry, June 26, 2003.

CHAPTER 10

DOG IS GOD SPELLED
BACKWARD

*He told another parable to them: "The kingdom of heaven is like a
mustard seed that someone took and planted in his field. It's the smallest
of all seeds. But when it's grown, it's the largest of all vegetable plants. It
becomes a tree so that the birds in the sky come and nest in its branches." He told them another parable: "The kingdom of heaven is like yeast,
which a woman took and hid in a bushel of wheat flour until the yeast
had worked its way through all the dough."*
—Matthew 13:31-33

*"To make bread or love, to dig in the earth, to feed an animal or cook
for a stranger—these activities require no extensive commentary,
no lucid theology. All they require is someone willing to
bend, reach, chop, stir."*
—Barbara Brown Taylor

It was a lazy, rainy fall day. Mom loaded me and my nephew, Joe, in the car and drove us to a nearby park loaded with big trees. (I have a nephew my age because Mom and Sister were pregnant at the same time. Awkward, but ultimately fun.)

We were seven years old. Joe often spent the night with Mom, which gave me the bonus of an extra sibling my age and untold adventures that, to this day, are our own sweet history: walking the woods, climbing stuff, skipping rocks, picking garden vegetables, going to the junkyard with my stepdad, shooting my BB gun at cans, and looking for turtles in creeks.

Because of the light rain that day, we were seekers under a shedding canopy of fall color, which was a striking view. As we walked across the wet ground, Mom encouraged us to find and collect our favorite leaves, whatever enchanted us. We meandered slowly, poking with the toes of our tennis shoes, to work at uncovering colors and patterns. There was an astonishing vibrancy to the damp bits of leftover glory yielded by an oak or elm: buttery yellow, tawny, pumpkin orange, cardinal, and soft wine. It was not surprising to see crumpled brown leaves, but, on this day, they seemed to recede in reverence to the vibrancy of color. We felt the slow, steady droplets of water from the leaves above, their stems yet to let go. Still, we kept our eyes to the earth and the bed of fall below our feet, the only noise being our slow footsteps treading along a trail of beauty. We stepped gingerly, then, when inspired, bent down carefully to scoop a leaf that could not be ignored.

Once we got back to the house with our collection, Mom pulled out the wax paper, set up the ironing board, and plugged in her iron. She invited us to arrange our leaves across the wax paper, then she placed another sheet on top of our design. She pressed the two sides together with the heat of the iron, making our patterns into a collage. After cooling them, Mom displayed our stained glass leaves.

In her book *Altar in the World*, Barbara Brown Taylor notices that children are very near the earth and know how to walk the earth because they notice stuff that many of us big people forget, so tied are we to our cell phones, our purses, our own thoughts and preoccupied with the concerns of tomorrow. A child, she says, can feel the heat from the sidewalk, can hear the tapping of her shoes on cement, notices a dime dropped in the crosswalk; a child is so near to the earth that a small acorn underfoot might topple her.

Tending children and watching them grow helps one remember a closeness to the earth: noticing leaves that have fallen, a roly poly bug under a rock, moss on a log, a dandelion puffball to blow; playing in the rain or a luscious puddle that has collected; and creating a happy oasis for feet to splash.

And, yes, children also notice the underbelly too, such as the mole that popped up on our older doggie's head. "It could be a tick," said Aubrey, as he parted her hair with his fingers for a closer inspection, wanting to nurture and care for her. Or the traumatic time (or two or three times) that our beloved Pointer escaped the backyard and scared us all to death because we couldn't catch her. At one point we caught sight of her in a neighbor's yard, chasing a buck. The boys were in panic mode. There were tears and even some wailing. I had to say to them, "I think she will come home." I couldn't say I was certain she'd return. My Sisters, we need to let the young ones learn about things that wow us and scare us; the mysteries of life are woven into the earth God has given us.

All Children Need Kindergarten

Humbly, may I suggest that kindergarten has become disconnected from its original meaning? Somehow in our American culture, what should be tiny people's time for exploring the world has become too often about pushing these delicate seedlings further into adulthood. I'm not sure I'm on board with rigorous standards and goals that seem suited to a more mature audience, like the bigger kids who are not so keen anymore on dressing up as a policeman or singing along with Thomas the Train.

Kindergarten is a German word that is translated "garden for children." I'm all about that word in its original meaning. Only in the last few years—and I'm sad to admit it—have I celebrated that I'm a growing work in progress.

As a plant in a larger garden, I've got some growing to do. Imagine that! I've had my share of blight, failure to thrive, curling leaves, and neglect (mostly of my own creation), and yep, I've even been trampled by others. Sisters, this awareness means that I now intentionally admit to my kids that I'm not done growing. I tell them that growth is a big renegade choice because I want them to be open to change, to transformation, to exploration without the fear of getting it wrong. Wrong is opportunity, not a forever-state to be lived in.

I once saw a magnet with a quote by the twentieth-century artist Pablo Picasso: "It takes a long time to grow young." I don't know precisely what Pablo meant, but I translate the wisdom of those words in my own spiritual way as, "Get past your need to know it all, past your desire for accomplishments, past your need to have it all together. Don't hide from the light where reality can be seen, even your own faults. Be born again. Let the Spirit blow you where it will. Listen to the wind" (see John 3:1-8).

When I was seven years old, Mom was newly divorced. We lived in a nice but tiny rental house on a hilly street. Before serious recreational biking or 10K races were popular, Mom used Saturday housework, some gardening, and walking our block to stretch her legs and mine.

Over the big hill at the end of the street was a small piece of heaven on earth. For the owners of the lot, it wasn't merely pretty grass, I'm sure. It was their meticulously tended lawn. I could have cared less about the official variety of deepest green grass, which I'd never seen before; it was a carpet. Each time we passed the house, I looked around to avoid trouble, then waited for Mom's nod. I ran full-born into the yard, laid down, and moved my arms and legs to create angel wings, as if I had fallen on a bank of fresh snow. Strikingly green, the millions of soft blades smelled delicious and were, what I imagined they would be, cloud-soft. The psalmist noticed the spiritual connection between God's care and lying upon the earth: "[The shepherd] lets me rest in grassy meadows" (Psalm 23:2).

When I was a child, being outdoors slowly revealed the language of something bigger than I was.

The first real garden Mom and I created was only a few years later. By that summer, I'd finished fifth grade. Mom was dating a kind man named Pete, who'd grown up in a poor family. They had no indoor plumbing and picked cotton for a living. He never wanted to pick cotton again, but he loved to grow gardens. He tilled a patch of ground for us in a corner of the backyard. Mom and I began our work with plants and seeds. We had seeds for tomatoes, cucumbers, beans, peppers, and squash. I desperately wanted to plant asparagus, so Mom purchased the seeds. Once our rectangular patch was freshly turned toward the black soil, we put our seeds in the ground.

I was proud when my ferny-looking plants began to grow. I dreamed of seeing the long stems of asparagus, picking them, and eating them. There are, however, times in your life when, if you are lucky, you begin to understand that not everything will happen when you believe it should happen or want it to happen. Life disciplines us. I was full-on disappointed when I learned that the asparagus plant takes about three years to mature enough to bear the luscious green stalks that are ready to eat. Three years seemed an eternity to an eleven-year-old.

Later that summer, Mom married Pete. The plan was to move to his home, a modest house he'd built, which sat on almost one full acre of land. I was devastated at the thought of leaving behind my asparagus, so Pete carefully uprooted my plants and relocated them to his massive garden. My beloved asparagus survived the transplant. By the third year, Pete announced the asparagus was ready to be picked. For years, each spring, that asparagus sprouted its green beginnings, grew tall and wispy, and gave us real-deal asparagus. I had never seen it outside a can. Patience and slowly maturation—these are the revelations of growing gardens.

Settled in this new life with a bigger yard, I watched my sweet Momma plant her own favorites. She had pampas grass lining the drive-way. Now when I see the newer, endless grasses around my town, in yards, and around businesses, I think Mom would love them. Her love of poinsettias led Pete to build a heated greenhouse, which also helped with early spring plants. Mom also got a few fig bushes, whose leaves, I discovered, are scratchy. I was finally able to grasp the sad hilarity of the first man and woman in the garden that God gave them, pitifully sewing together scratchy fig leaves to cover their poor choices. Separating ourselves from God is so miserable.

My parents were local foodies before it was hip. They had survived the Great Depression, and Mom wouldn't tolerate a finicky eater. My niece says she'd never know the joys of pressure-cooked greens if Meemaw hadn't made her eat them. From the time of that first garden that Mom and I planted in the back of our rented house, my summers included a kitchen full of vegetables lined up along counters and windowsills. Window units couldn't keep up with the hot steam of the old pressure cooker and the canning chores, but in winter, we had a taste of the summer: green beans, pickled cucumbers and okra, tomatoes, corn relish, and syrupy strawberry preserves. The old pear tree's fruit was tough when picked fresh, but with cinnamon and sugar, Mom's canned pears were yum-yum.

After a busy and hot day in the canning kitchen, we rested. Hearing the intermittent ping of the full Kerr jars was a kind of music for those who know that the preparation, the work, the effort is now blessed. Well done, good and faithful servant. Remember the summer, the garden, its smell and taste, its sacred fruit and lessons. Pass the deep burgundy chunks of strawberry, straight from the gifted Preservestress: "Taste and see how good the LORD is!" (Psalm 34:8a).

Move Through the Earth

When I was a child, being outdoors slowly revealed the language of something bigger than I was, something that helped me see myself and all of us humans as part of a larger world to explore. We often neglect the impact of the natural world and its potential to transform.

When I began to read chapter books to Penn, one of the first we read was the English classic *The Secret Garden*. Little and sickly Mary Lennox is born into a wealthy family. She is spoiled, neglected, and often left alone. When she loses her parents in a cholera epidemic, she is moved into Misselthwaite Manor with her wealthy and absent uncle. Mary discovers a dormant garden walled off and forgotten. As the unhappy and emotionally stunted girl visits and tends the garden secretly with a farm boy, its rejuvenation begins to heal Mary and her sickly, unhappy cousin, Colin.

Sisters, in my tradition, God took on flesh and walked the earth, picking wheat grains, talking of sowing seeds and yeast that rises and vines and the vineyards they come from and weeds and fish and sheep and even dogs. God, as one of us, climbed mountains, swam, and sat in boats and by lakes. This embrace of the creation is an example of what we, too, need. Being aware of the creation around us is one of the gifts God has given us for wholeness.

One of my brothers, Tom, who was sixteen when I was born, raised beagles to hunt with. I loved the litters of white-and-lemon-colored puppies. Soft fur, milky breath, closed eyes. Tom also brought home fish to clean and cook. He took me sledding, boating, camping, fishing, and swimming at nearby lakes. There was nothing quite like the exhausted feeling of a long day outside. Even after a rare day of biting cold in the South and peeling off wet clothes because there were no Polartec fabrics, my body felt satisfied. Or the times I'd come home with my ponytail matted after hours of swimming, the wind having blown against my face through the car windows all the way home. It was a good tired. I see it in my children when we foster their outdoor adventures, whether it is a bike ride around the block or a day of hiking the woods or picking up trash at the river park.

My uncle Paul and aunt Mary owned a rather ramshackle farm

> *Let them slice the onion (with supervision), let them cry, let their eyes burn, and then hand them a paper towel.*

and raised horses. As we walked through the barn one day and I watched my uncle tend the horses, he promised, "I'm going to make you a horse woman." I was so excited and so scared because I knew nothing about horses except they were absolutely beautiful. He died when I was seven, but I'd already gotten my shoes dirty at their old dilapidated place, ate the fried eggs cooked on my aunt's old stove, hunted Easter eggs near the barn, sat on the old tractor, and fell in love with the horse trough. And then there were the family legends that were passed down: an enormous snake skin found draped on the branches of a giant oak near the old farmhouse and that time my mom was eaten alive with chiggers while picking blackberries and then kicked over her bucket when she saw a snake. I felt a deep loss when my uncle died, an ache of regret that I missed learning a very important language. I'm not a real cowgirl, but I have a serious collection of boots.

Not long ago, we took our four boys on a trail ride. It wasn't an extreme, daredevil experience, but they had to keep their feet in the stirrups, handle the reins, hear about the wild hogs that roamed the area at night, watch how close the horses' feet came to the edge of a narrow and higher path, and sit in a place they'd never been before, which can later feel like a pain in the butt. I'm talking saddle sore.

Let them get sore, tired, scared, nervous. Let them struggle with new stuff, without my hovering over their possible missteps. Let them get their hands very dirty, let their feet go bare, watch them fry an egg. Let them slice the onion (with supervision), let them cry, let their eyes burn, and then hand them a paper towel. *These things happen,* you say, *but wait until you smell this punishing vegetable sautéing with butter and garlic. Child, you will thank God.*

That's the way I felt when I got brave and bought lettuce plants. When they were ready, I showed the boys how to chop off the leaves. I placed the vivid green leaves in my bright red colander to wash them. I stared at the little bundle with pride and admiration, not because I'd grown them, but because God was in that moment of creativity, food, and nourishment for the spirit.

Nurture Something with Your Kids

For years the matriarchs of the family grew a plant they called "devil's back," short for "devil's backbone." It's considered a subtropical succulent with variegated leaves. My mom was rather nutty about her devil's back and proudly offered cuttings as if she were sharing sourdough starter. It was a thing to get a cutting and have your own plant, and there are still plants from her original growing in all my siblings' homes. That may be about forty years of plant.

Watching people grow stuff is important. I've already mentioned the way I learned, but I believe nurture and empathy go together. You have to cultivate these traits. Loving God and loving neighbor isn't a suggestion; it's a necessity for us to grow beyond ourselves. And I feel certain God didn't place us in a garden to ignore the plants and animals. *Here, name this thing!* said God (see Genesis 2:18-25). I know that naming each of my children was an intimate act; it connected them to me and to our family, especially since we chose family names. I started a relationship of love and care before I held a baby in my arms.

I love dogs. In my kitchen, there is a small sign on a shelf that says, "Dog Hair: Both a Condiment and a Fashion Accessory." Maybe you're not a "dog whisperer," but let your kids try giving to someone, especially after they begin to wean from their cherished lovie.

One of our boy's pre-K teachers had a bearded dragon named Hazel in her classroom. Wyatt was in love with Hazel. She even wore clothes and came to our animal blessing at the church. I blessed a bearded dragon—in clothes. The next year, Wyatt's new teacher had a baby bearded dragon that the class called Flame. There has been a strong and steady request from Wyatt and Aubrey for a bearded dragon in our home. I don't know. Flame's keeper said the reptile isn't that tough: she's afraid of dead mice. That means more trips to the pet grocery for grasshoppers. I can barely keep enough food for school lunches.

Along with our dogs, cats, and my husband's fish, we've planted tons of milkweed plants in our yard to attract monarch butterflies, whose population has declined by 80 percent from their peak in 1997. Our boys have learned to spot the monarch caterpillar, collect the leaves, and feed them until they form a chrysalis at the top of the critter keeper. The boys get to watch them emerge completely different, totally transformed.

Relationships Transform Us

When we adopted our Pointer, I noticed she had an unfortunate habit of sucking on cushions, pillows, and throws. She not only sucked on the fabric but also nibbled tiny bits of cloth at the corners and made holes. *Great*, I thought. *Just what we needed. A new family member who likes to destroy stuff.*

I knew she'd been found near Lake Norrell, half-starved and flea-bitten. Whether she'd been dropped, was gun-shy and bolted, or was on a wild run and got lost, we'd probably never know, but it was clear she needed someone to find her. I'd never had an adult dog who chewed, so I called one of my friends who's a dog whisperer and asked her what might be bothering this sweet girl. She told me that dogs will suck and nibble as a result of stress, so the answer was love and affection. Nori was shy about eating and was not a dominant dog. Over time, we coaxed her with food and gave her plenty of space. Gradually, this forty-pound dog would sit in my lap, cuddle, stare at me with her honey-gold eyes, and shed on me with her gorgeous white and chocolate coat.

Nori doesn't suck on the furniture anymore. I think she knows she's home. I call her Nori-ella. I didn't really adopt her; she adopted me. She keeps me from chewing holes in the pillows too.

Notes

Barbara Brown Taylor, *An Altar in the World* (New York: HarperOne, 2009), xviii and 62–63.

CHAPTER 11

WOMENADE: SO THAT HAPPENED

*Ask, and you will receive. Search, and you will find. Knock, and the
door will be opened to you. For everyone who asks, receives. Whoever
seeks, finds. And to everyone who knocks, the door is opened.*
—Matthew 7:7-8

*We are the champions, my friends
And we'll keep on fighting 'til the end.*
—Queen

It was the best of times. It was the worst of times. OK, I borrowed that famous opening. Thank you, Charles Dickens, for setting up the description of my disappointment. You are the patron saint of hardships, like debtor's prison. (Please don't tell my husband I recently bought two more pillow covers from Pottery Barn.)

Each year, I plan a family beach getaway. Water is my thing. I crave it. I was born under a water sign, cancer the crab, and one of my besties was too. She embraces the crab and swears by beach rejuvenation as an annual pilgrimage. Of course, shells, water, and getting soaked is also a sign of new life for us Christians.

I make reservations several months in advance somewhere on the gulf coast around the long stretch of road known as 30A, which is advertised on bumper stickers affixed to the backs of mom cars across the south, whispering, *I was there, Sister, and I'm going again.* It's a twelve-hour jaunt with four kids, although our friends swear it only takes ten hours. As with most vacations, our family thinks about it, talks about it, and looks forward to it—for months. We've made some big, beautiful memories along the seashore, and we've had a few *Oh, wells.*

I've thought a lot about why I love the beach. Maybe it's the hypnotic sound of the waves going in and out, which is not too far removed from what you hear when the doctor lets you hear the swishing noise going on in your pregnant belly. My affection for the beach may also include imagining Jesus hanging out along the shore with his friends, grilling a day's catch. I admit I didn't think about Jesus as much when

I was spring-breaking with my college girlfriends. *Jesus, I'm just being honest. I was young and thought more of myself than you.* Maybe my love of our annual beach trip also has to do with cleansing because I'm forced to simplify in a small rental condo and get in really close quarters with my people. I once read that an early Christian said if God is at the center of the circle, and we are all around the circle, then the closer we get to one another, the closer we get to God. I bet that early Christian didn't have four boys. Another possibility for my love of the beach pilgrimage is that the sand and water are my Protestant-girl Lourdes.

One of our more recent beach trips was lousy. I'm calling it. Straight up. It did not conform to my standards. At all.

Two significant events happened the month before we left for Beachdom, which already put me under stress—more stress than the children's summer schedules and running a house in which the laundry is downstairs and the three bedrooms are upstairs.

There were obviously bigger, more important fish to fry than my silly beach inconveniences.

1. I had unexpected hernia surgery a month before we left.

2. I began a new ministry job the week before the hernia surgery.

These events, plus a looming school year with four kids, made my longing for salt life even greater.

The first day on the beach, as always, we lathered with sunscreen. In particular, I need it because I'm a very white girl. The second day, I noticed my lower legs were itching, so I put a towel over them. I'm way past wanting a suntan, and fake-and-bake lotion is my reliable friend.

That evening, I came in and showered. My husband noticed a rash on my upper arms. My legs felt prickly too. I had what appeared to be blood blisters below the skin of my ankles and one knee. The itching that night was so horrendous. I barely slept. Benadryl and hydrocortisone didn't touch it. Aloe gave it a really good team try.

On day three, I stayed inside, miserable. That night, Sister arrived with her husband. They watched the boys while we went to a walk-in clinic. I got a steroid shot and a dose pack. I slept. Oh, did I sleep.

For the rest of our vacation, it rained. This rain was like nothing I'd ever experienced at the beach. It sprinkled lightly, and then suddenly it fell in sheets. There were storms almost every night. Lightning is very pretty—at home. Naturally, I barely slept those following nights because I was jacked up on steroids. Almost every day, two red flags were hoisted on the beach, warning everyone not to get in the water. The waves were outright hostile. I can't believe we paid money for this trip tragedy that I assumed would be 85 percent perfect.

And then there was the day my husband helped pull a thirteen-year-old boy, who was wearing a life jacket, from under the rolling waves. Victor signaled to a woman back on the shore who was watching the disturbing scene. He put a thumb and pinky to his head, the international "call me" sign. She understood and immediately dialed 911. By the time Victor and the boy's father brought him to sandy, dry land, the boy was unresponsive. Thankfully, he had a pulse and, in a few minutes, woke up, but his breathing was irregular. After the paramedics got there, they sent him on to the hospital.

A day later, we were still thinking about the boy. There were obviously bigger, more important fish to fry than my silly beach inconveniences.

On day five, my niece Kelly arrived with her boyfriend, Rob. They love to cook. After discussing some food ideas inclusive of children, they came back that night with fresh and plump boiled shrimp, some spicy, some plain. They prepared garlic bread, salad, corn, and pota-toes. Sister had made a pan of brownies earlier in the day. We filled and passed plates to one another and refilled. We talked and laughed and ate.

I was reminded of the final story in John's Gospel, the one in which the disciples clearly feel lost without Jesus (see John 21). They can't even catch real fish anymore. And then this guy appears on the beach and offers instruction as they slog around in the boat. It is only at that point the disciples catch a huge, net-straining load. Afterward, they sit around a charcoal grill and eat, and then they recognize Jesus. In the communion of eating together we see Jesus best and, likewise, who we're meant to be: people who care and nurture one another beyond ourselves. That's why Jesus tells Peter, "Go feed my sheep."

Of course I needed and wanted some time to unwind, but when I saw the father of the boy who almost drowned grab my husband's hand and grasp his shoulder in the way that men do when they might other-wise hug, I was glad we were there in this maddening weather, which is another thing I cannot control. "Feed my sheep" means "Be the next of kin whatever the circumstances because we're all family."

The day before we left, I'd scheduled a photographer to take family pics. She called the shoot done when the rain hit within minutes of our big family getting down to the beach. I told her to send any pictures that *might* be decent. In the four photos she e-mailed me, we look damp, happy, relaxed, and fed. And we were. I will never forget the hard-luck, beautiful-on-the-inside vacation.

You know what I call that perspective? I call that "womenade" because when our women plans crash and things go sour, God calls us to get creative and see life as a pitcher full, though sometimes tart.

Not What We Want, but What We Need

Recently, I traveled to a clergywoman thingy in Houston with a group of younger women from my state. I didn't know some of them well, so I offered to drive my van because it was an opportunity to make new friends. I thought about flying, just doing my own deal, which is sort of what I wanted to do. It'd be nice to be anonymous and avoid church talk. In the end, I decided it might be an adventure, if the young ones could tolerate my back-in-the-old-days-when-I-first-started-out-in-ministry stories. I promised not to tap them on the shoulder with my cane.

Guess what? I learned so much. They are wiser and more savvy than I was when I began pastoral ministry.

We not only attended the conference and visited tons but also, one afternoon, took an excursion in the big city, enjoying a wee bit of retail therapy. We went to the Kendra Scott jewelry store where there was a holiday sale. It was way groovy. Next we stopped by a toy store so I could take home some Legos for my boys, sick woman that I am. Then—and I was jumping up and down—we went to Trader Joe's grocery and bought cookie butter, dark chocolate espresso beans, and plantain chips. Some food just screams heaven.

All that was great, and a few of the conference preachers rocked; but the better part, as Jesus might say, was to sit in a car for close to sixteen hours and share our lives over cheddar puffs and food we brought and bought. And there was this mystical time, OMG, that Lynn said she wanted a DQ. Behold! Surely it was a sign! Yes, it was a DQ sign in the sky. We made a hasty left turn. I expect big things from the squad. On that long, tiring trip with these fabulous young women called by God, I wasn't sure what to pray for, what to search for, since I was conflicted about how this trip should go, control freak that I am. But, I asked God

153

Jesus, who loved perfectly, had his haters too. And his job wasn't to please people but to reveal God.

to figure it out, and God gave me what I needed.

My experience reminds me of the time Jesus said that we should ask and expect we'll receive (see Matthew 7:7-12). I'm not sure women are very good at asking, since we often ask everyone else what we need to do for them.

For a long time, I didn't like this passage of suspicious scripture *at all* because I've asked in my nicest, humblest voice for stuff to unfold my way. So, isn't it a shock, I didn't get what I expected or, to be more exact, what I thought I wanted?

One day, Sister and I were talking about this annoying passage. We both raised our collective eyebrows and admitted that we were a bit more seasoned since our first, rather naive impression of the text's meaning. Of course, back in our younger days, we'd assumed it to be about God giving us mostly what we ask for if we just pester God enough and it's not offensive. Admittedly, the assumption about expecting God to give me my heart's desire always troubled me. Surely that's not what Jesus meant.

As my ideas about who Jesus was and is deepened beyond my own expectations, I realized how often we treat him as some hack magician to do our bidding. This great passage I now love is not—I'm willing to pinky-swear, Sisters—a sure-fire way to get God to do what you want. God loves us, yes, but relation with The Mystery presents the world in its own sweet, divine, revelatory way.

Try this interpretation on as a more fruitful and realistic translation.

We may ask God for what we want, of course, but Jesus includes that we must search, which means the asking should not be a blind "gimme" request. Perhaps *asking* God is the initial way of saying aloud what we want, so that we can determine if our request is truly what we need.

The *search* for what we want may indeed lead us to what we need. I think searching equals discernment. Searching can't be avoided, or we will rush the process.

Knocking on the door is, I'm pretty sure, listed last in Jesus's list because then, and only then, are we ready to take the initiative. We've done the proper soul-searching. Searching means we've taken the God whispers seriously before we tap on the door.

At different times in my life, I've screwed up the steps. I've gotten what I wanted or what I thought I wanted.

Once, I wanted to marry a certain man, but it became clear that he was not the partner I needed in my life. It was painful to GPS-style recalculate my spirit because it meant I had to change, allowing God to rework me as I moved forward.

Another time, I asked to serve a church I really wanted, but what I got from that church was not what I wanted, but what I needed: a great deal of discernment, introspection, and painful learning about where God really wanted me to be.

And, yes, I asked for children. That was a game changer but, on the whole, more like hitting the jackpot in Vegas, after which these tiny people below your waist ask you for a loan, like, every day.

Do I think of these challenges as my misfired, misguided asks? Do I wish I could take them back? Occasionally, it crosses my mind that I've bit off more than I can chew, but then I've also come to realize the paths I've chosen are hard-wired into my story. If only all of us women could shut down the negative talk that keeps us reliving mistakes in our heads, second-guessing ourselves. After one hard life lesson, my brother Steve said, "You know what they say? When God closes one door, nail that sucker shut!"

Amen.

We need to detach from what other people think and say about our marriage, our children, our parenting, and our work choices. Get an umbrella for the shade thrown your way. You know what I mean. Dry-erase that board in your head of the names and opinions of those who are always judging *your* life. Once, I heard someone had called me Betsy Barbie to demean me and my leadership, but that's OK because Barbie is ordained now—thank you, Mattel—and before that she was an astronaut. Reframing our painful experiences can be divine.

Jesus, who loved perfectly, had his haters too. And his job wasn't to please people but to reveal God. When humans discover God loves everyone, it's rather shocking because, *surely*, we have convinced ourselves, *God loves the most perfect, best, and all-together person in the room. All I must do is get me perfect.*

Think about that.

What if our personal choices, our challenges, our searching, our knocks on the door arose from our sacred calling to reveal, above all, the love of God, even for us? That might help us turn down our worry knob, stop pushing the button to gauge our popularity, or put away the tape measure that we use to decide if we're like the people whom we have convinced ourselves have it all together.

I'm not some Pollyanna Preacher. I don't believe Jesus's path is easy; but, as hard as it is to stumble and second-guess and suffer the consequences, there is still love. And somehow God doesn't seem to hold it against me or you when we have not searched and listened more before we ask. When I feel that gracious God love, I want to get a very big scripture tattoo somewhere on my body, but I think it's OK if I simply rewrite the God love (maybe in Sharpie) on my heart. That is probably enough.

Jesus, help me remember that you always help me discover what I truly need.

Everyone Screws Up

There are these unseemly bad-mom behaviors I want to take back after the fact but can't. Maybe you have some too. Sometimes I yell, which is not what I want to do or who I want to be. It's just that I sometimes feel like a carnival barker trying to get people who are ignoring the freak show to pay attention to my nifty, loud tricks. And let's be blunt. There are four growing boys in my home.

I really don't know how they got here, or, let's just say, some days it's rather foggy. Let me squint and think. My eyes aren't what they used to be even with my prescription-strength Ray Ban glasses. Thankfully, I've come to realize that it's not just seeing what's in front of me, but it's looking inside.

Yet I'd like to find an easy way to turn on the personal back-up camera. Looking behind at the past is a way to get prepared to move forward. You can't look behind you forever, but there are reasons I screw up, and I want to understand and do better. It's not just yelling at the boys, which, admittedly, turns me into the child. I've literally had a boy say, "Momma, just calm down. It's not that bad," to which I said, "And how did you get so grown up, for goodness sakes?"

At the end of a day, these kids prance gleefully through the house, or so it seems, when I'm tired or empty or vulnerable. Who said they could be so carefree? Who said they could throw towels and underwear with abandon? Who said they could leave chunks of toothpaste in the sink or help themselves to my ice cream? And that doesn't include the indignities they unknowingly call out.

Recently, I put my sleeveless arm around Sullivan on a hot summer day in the car while Dad drove. That sweet little boy smiled at me sheepishly. I smiled back, thinking he was happy just to sit next to me. "What is it, Honey?" I said, love sparkling from my eyes, making me warm and content. He said, "Momma, your armpit has a beard."

Are there no secrets?

I want to sit them down and say, "I have worked hard and done a million things today that you don't know about. I have coordinated all your activities, packed your lunch, tried to figure out how to get on this stupid app to see your homework status, loved a bunch of people on behalf of Jesus, and planned outreach that will knock your socks off, plus I washed your dang stinky socks, found your shoes in places you never could, fed the dogs, and washed the dishes. Yep, look at me, Little Man. I'm the 'shero' and don't forget it." I really want to say stuff like that, and I do sometimes. Sort of.

But my list of accomplishments essentially goes on the same shelf as yelling. I'm talking to me. These are my problems, not theirs.

It is absolutely true that they need to help get their laundry, carry their clothes to their upstairs rooms, put dirty dishes in the sink or dishwasher, teamwork stuff. But sometimes it seems easier to do it myself. Maybe—Lord, help me—I do it because I like to have control over the way it's done. I am pretty certain my way is best. Maybe it's because I'm not the best coach. I'm more of a vision person, so I'm thinking I know what this tidy life is supposed to look like, which is killer when you have boys who are fine with "good enough."

Geez, maybe it's because I'm not playing man-to-man but zone, and it's wearing me out. I'm an older mom. Please don't judge me because I bought some purple, gray, and fuchsia lipsticks recently. Maybe that's partly what Pablo meant. Don't be afraid of color. Parenting is not paint-by-numbers, and neither is faith and trust in God to walk with us when we are uncertain. Haven't you noticed how God likes to meander and take God's own sweet time? Revelation is not the same as WiFi.

On days when I've hit a wall or a vivid memory, I think of Mom. She wasn't perfect by any means. I see some of her shortcomings in myself: I am jealous, have a sharp tongue, am easily hurt, have a need for recognition, and act on gut instinct. But she hugged me often, told me she loved me, encouraged me far beyond my dreams, never told me I couldn't do anything, and very rarely judged.

There was that one time after my first year of college when I rolled in at two in the morning. As soon as I opened the door, she growled between clenched teeth, "I don't know who you think you are, but I'm not running a flophouse!" She set a boundary: "You are not going to use me for cheap meals and lodging." I loved the way Mom could roll her eyes with the smirk of a stand-up comedian. The thought of that single, hilarious look is like a drop of precious, scented oil on my secret shelf, to pull out and open occasionally. I breathe it in and rub it lovingly across my dry, aging hands that are starting to look like hers.

Mom, I cannot wait to tell my boys that I am absolutely not running a flophouse.

God Made Bossy Moms

So don't think that Jesus's mother didn't lose it, because she did. I wish she'd kept a journal because we've only got a few pages of the photo album in the Gospels, but that's enough for us to consider.

Luke gives Mary more ink than the rest of the New Testament writers. He gives us long scenes of Mary and the angel who comes with a message from God. Mary wonders. Mary ponders. She ponders when the angel approaches her, when the shepherds arrive under the stars of night to repeat the angels' glad tidings. She ponders when her child is presented in the temple and Simeon blesses them. She ponders as she watches her child grow up.

I have a picture in our bedroom, a rather large pastel drawing of the angel Gabriel as a woman. There is no picture of Mary, only the angel bending down and extending a lily to the woman beyond the picture. While I'm not concerned about angelic gender, I sensed the artist was saying that perhaps this particular angel could have appeared as a woman to announce a particular kind of motherhood, woman to woman.

The anemone, the flower most artists have put in this annunciation scene, was probably the most rich and bountiful wildflower in the fields and hillsides of Palestine. This flower was easily picked and offered up as a symbol of how much God loves the smallest of details, including, I think, *our* details, the times women grapple with best practices and ways to organize and embrace our messy selves and families (see Luke 12:27-31). Maybe each of us moms needs to embrace this angelic messenger who extends a lily, an invitation, a gift to remind us what is important when we embark upon a life of mothering.

Pondering accompanies joy. Yes, we know Mary rejoiced with her pregnant kin Elizabeth, singing that radical song, the Magnificat, a song not about what Mary's child would do for her or about the maternal role he would give her, but what this child would be for others, for the whole world. I don't see Mary as a passive figure; she's a bossy momma.

Mary is going to be there, to be present for her child on a very long journey, from birth announcement to ascension and beyond. From the beginning it's not easy: a doubtful fiancé, a barnyard birth, even a nighttime escape to Egypt to protect the child from Herod (Matthew 2:13-15).

Imagine her thoughts the time young Jesus disappears. Mary can do without her son's quiet departure from their large caravan when he treks all the way back to the temple in Jerusalem. After locating him, she looks her rabbinical prodigy in the face and says, "Son, why have you scared us to death? You listen to me! Your dad and I have been worried sick. We've been looking everywhere for you!" (Luke 2:48, my paraphrase) Mary says, "Excuse me, I'm not running a flophouse!" This is not the first or only time Mary's son will brush her off and begin, as all children do, to claim their own calling.

When Mary's host instinct kicks in at a wedding, she asks her son to do something about the wine, which is running low (see John 2:1-12). He balks, but I picture her pulling her son in a corner and saying, "Now you listen to me. This is about generosity and hospitality." Boom. And maybe Mary was also thinking about how long she'd been waiting for him to show the world what he was born to do.

When Mary seems concerned about the crowd with which Jesus is associating, when she tries to bring him home from this open-door ministry, he announces within earshot that blood does not determine family. Jesus says that doing the will of God alone makes us family (see Matthew 12:48; Luke 8:21; and Mark 3:33). I bet she pondered that little zinger for quite some time. Oh how children can pierce your heart.

Still, I see Mary always near, as most mothers are, wondering how this story is going to end. Bless her. She's there until the end and beyond. As her son is executed, she stands at the foot of his horrible cross. Jesus tells her she has a new son, who is the disciple standing next to her, and, amazingly, this beloved disciple has a new mother (see John 19:25-27). Mary gave her child life, and now he gives her a son.

Following Jesus's death and resurrection, Mary is still there at the ascension of that child she once held in her arms. At this point, the story gets very personal. Letting go is hard work. Of course she knew he was going to grow beyond her. She'd been told from the very beginning that her son was going to be a gift to the world, but it's different when the day to say good-bye finally arrives. She looks up into the sky, and it's hard to look away, even after she can no longer see him, like the glow that follows after the flash of a camera. All that is left are two men clothed in white, who tell the followers it is time to move ahead together. So they make their way back to an upstairs room to pray and to wait for the Spirit of God to pour itself upon all people who might now, finally, understand one another and the meaning of one big God family.

And, in my imagination, Mary ponders again what has happened and what might happen next, as all responsible mothers do, always and forever. We ponder and wait and hope.

What we get is not always what we want, but what we most need is making it through the hard and fun stuff that happens in our families, that crazy, messy tangled ball of people who are learning to practice forgiveness, grace, and love. Over and over again we practice because it never goes according to plan. Thank God.

ACKNOWLEDGMENTS

MY CUP RUNNETH OVER
BECAUSE GOD GAVE US
A SQUAD

My family and this book would never have happened without the hilarity of a surprising God who has provided more hands than I have, more hope than I have, and more love than I have. My nice jeans have stylish holes in the knees from prostrate thanks for what and *who* has happened in our lives since Abraham and Sarah had Isaac (Laughter), then, in minute succession, Giggle, Snort, and Are You Kidding Me?

From the time Victor and I brought our triplets home, people we knew—and many we didn't—came to our rescue. We survived and thrived because people loved us.

Husband, thank you for making my dreams come true. Without my cheerleaders, Sister Gayle and Friend Gayle, my sanity would be in question and this book would not exist. Without Friend Dale's wisdom, I would wander in the wilderness.

Thank you forever.

ACKNOWLEDGMENTS

And if I mistakenly left you off, I will be mortified when we next run into each other because I have manners.

Abingdon Team: Susan Salley for those first conversations. Dawn Woods and Susan Cornell for patience and direction.

The Squad

The fab schools and teachers
Judy Adams and crew
Terry and Gary* Barket (grace in the flesh)
Rhonda Bensen
Whitney Bordelon and family
Angie Bowden and Sarah Johnson (and Greenbay)
Nancy Campalans
Betty Chadduck (Suga, your hot fudge forever!)
Tom* and Frances Chaffin
Araya Charles
Lacey Chavez
The Congressional staffs of Vic Snyder, DC and Little Rock
Suzanne Coulter (Only you could teach the Razorback fight song.)
Dr. Lynn Davis
Jo DeWitt (through babies and fur ...)
Renee and Dr. John Dickens
Kearney and Floy Jean* Dietz
Karen, Steve, and Sara Doty (Keep the cookies coming, Aunt Karen!)
Lindsey Eidt
Dr. Betty Everett
Paul and Gayle Fiser with Mabel Harris Webb* (not without prayer)

Gayle and Jerry Gardner (always faithful)
Kelly, Matt, and Joe Gardner
Lisa Ledbetter Gerhardt
Judy Gribble
Greer Griebel
Linda and Mollie Halbrook
Lawrence Hamilton*
Suzanne Hamilton
Ashley Haning
Maria and Ignacio Heurta
Dr. Charlotte Hobbs and Benjamin Robbins
Mark Hotchkiss
Dr. Cindy Hubach
Dixie Knight* (thanks for the memories)
Lynn Knight
Jill, Jack, and Caroline Lawrence
Nancy Ledbetter
Jon and Sandra Marbaise
Rev. Michael Mattox
Nancy McCulley
Catie Mitchell
Cindy and Chip Murphy
Marilyn Myatt
Kristin Vandaveer Nicholson
Bobbye Nixon
Paul and Becky Owen
Judy and Thomas Owens
Peeraya "Poom" Peters
Pulaski Heights UMC
Quapaw Quarter UMC

Dr. Chad Rogers and LR Pediatric
Carly Roitz and her parents
Dale Rowett
Kate, Mary, and Melinda* Sain (pedicures and Mexican food)
Becky and Steve Singleton (would never have made it without you)
Jack and Susie Singleton (Saturdays and books)
Tom and D. Gayle Singleton (porches and more)
Dr. Kathy Smith and Kaitlin Smith Long
Charles Stanley
Anne Teeter
Trinity UMC
Linda Tullos
The United Methodist Church of the Resurrection
UAMS NICU and OB Staffs
Jo Lynn Varner
Shay Watson
Kim Whetstone
Amanda White
Lisa Baldridge Williams
Myron Yancey
Jan Zimmerman
Nancy Zotz, Jayme Moberly, and Chad Cornelius

*Friends we have lost and love

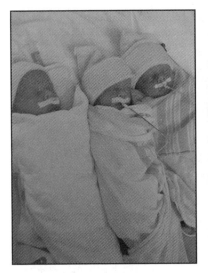

Baby triptych, one toddler, and the chart that kept us sane.

Photos above and below courtesy Dixie Knight Photography

Top left: Yes, we have our hands full! *Top right and right*: A sweet and exhausting family photo shoot. *Below*: Visiting with Rep. Nancy Pelosi at the White House picnic.

Clockwise from top: The heavenly host was too bright for some. Going hiking. Cooking with Aunt Gayle. Loving the great outdoors.

4043

We wouldn't change a thing, but there *were* a gazillion diapers.